THE SQUIGGLY CAREER

'A brilliant guide. Read it and get the tools you need to thrive
in your career now and in the future'
**MARIE FORLEO, NUMBER ONE *NEW YORK TIMES* BESTSELLING
AUTHOR OF *EVERYTHING IS FIGUREOUTABLE***

'Many of us never take a moment to think about how we can sculpt our careers to
match our interests. I was swept away with how effortlessly *The Squiggly Career* turns
some of the most daunting conundrums into simple and rewarding reflections'
BRUCE DAISLEY, AUTHOR OF *THE JOY OF WORK*

'A practical and excellent guide for anyone who wants to take charge of their career,
play to their strengths and design a career on their own terms. Squiggly careers
are the new normal indeed. I'll be reaching for this book time and time again and
so wish it existed when I started out!'
ELIZABETH UVIEBINENÉ, AUTHOR OF *SLAY IN YOUR LANE*

'The greatest goal for any 21st-century professional is to have a squiggly career.
The days of linear progression belong to history. The joys of trying new things,
working it out and making it up are all of our working futures. Work is dead,
long live the squiggly career!'
SAM CONNIFF ALLENDE, AUTHOR OF *BE MORE PIRATE*

'All the best careers are squiggly. That sounds fun – and it can be fun – but it also
takes a lot of know-how and thinking, which is what this book provides. I wish I'd had
it when I squiggled my way through multiple careers and I already know dozens of
people of all ages whom it will help'
MARGARET HEFFERNAN, AUTHOR OF *WILFUL BLINDNESS*

'*The Squiggly Career* is no ordinary business book. Practical, pithy and personal, it will revolutionize the way you think about work'

CRYSTAL EISINGER, HEAD OF STRATEGY, GOOGLE ADS MARKETING

'A fantastic book on how to maximize your chances of a happy and rewarding work life. It all starts with knowing yourself and your values – with simple exercises that make you think deeply about who you are and what you want to spend all that time at work actually doing. Jump in and squiggle'

MATT BRITTIN, PRESIDENT, EMEA BUSINESS AND OPERATIONS, GOOGLE

The Squiggly Career

Ditch the Ladder
Discover Opportunity
Design Your Career

Helen Tupper and Sarah Ellis

BUSINESS

PENGUIN BUSINESS

UK | USA | Canada | Ireland | Australia
India | New Zealand | South Africa

Penguin Business is part of the Penguin Random House group of companies
whose addresses can be found at global.penguinrandomhouse.com.

Penguin
Random House
UK

First published 2020
001

Copyright © Helen Tupper and Sarah Ellis, 2019

The moral right of the authors has been asserted

Text design and typesetting by Couper Street Type Co.
Printed and bound in Great Britain by Clays Ltd, Elcograf S.p.A.

A CIP catalogue record for this book is available from the British Library

ISBN: 978–0–241–38584–5

Follow us on LinkedIn: linkedin.com/company/penguinbusiness

www.greenpenguin.co.uk

For Gareth and Tom, whose unwavering support
makes everything possible.

And for Henry, Madeleine and Max
for making us laugh (and cry) along the way.

Contents

Welcome to your squiggly career

We're going to start by asking you three questions about your career today:

1. Do you feel like you're climbing a ladder with each step of your career clearly mapped out ahead of you?
2. Can you imagine working in the same role for the next five years, and in the same company for the next ten?
3. Do you think you'll be able to retire at the same age as your parents?

No, no and *unlikely!* are the typical responses that most people give to these questions.

The world of work has changed dramatically over the last few decades and for the most part it's changed for the better. Today, careers are filled with endless opportunities, but those opportunities also come with more complications. Most of us are seeking jobs that excite and fulfil us, where we can use our strengths, find purpose, work flexibly and learn new skills. We've come to expect a lot from our careers, and are constantly told to 'love your job', 'follow your dreams' and 'live your best life'. But this aspirational advice often feels far removed from our reality. Sometimes it's hard to 'follow your dreams' when you have rent or a mortgage to pay, a manager to keep happy and expectations from colleagues and friends that you should be available on email or WhatsApp 24/7.

> Jobs for life are a thing of the past and our career expectations have changed.

There's a gap between the promise of work today – a shiny world full of opportunity, creativity and freedom – and the reality of many people's careers. And building the bridge to this new world of work is going to take more than pithy advice and inspirational quotes.

So, what does it take? To find happiness in the modern world of work and take control of your career now and in the future, you need to develop a set of five career skills. These skills are:

1. **Super Strengths: the things you are great at.** You need to know what your strengths are and take action to make sure your strengths stand out across everything you do.

2. **Values: what makes you 'you'.** Identifying what motivates and drives you will help you make the right career decisions and understand other people in a meaningful way.

3. **Confidence: belief in yourself.** We all have 'confidence gremlins', the things that hold us back at work. You can learn how to cage these gremlins and build your resilience by focusing on your successes and developing a strong support system.

4. **Networks: people helping people.** It is important to build relationships in a way that works for you, and to learn to build an effective network based on what you can give rather than gain.

5. **Future Possibilities: exploring options.** Career plans are a thing of the past; your focus should be on identifying future possibilities and taking action to explore them in the present. What is your work 'why' and how can it help futureproof your career now?

It is within everyone's capability and control to develop these skills no matter what stage of your career you are at – whether you've just started out in your first job, are a manager leading a team of ten people, or have just launched your own business.

Knowing and using your strengths, living your values, caging your confidence gremlins, building a network in a way that works for you and exploring

> Ditch the ladder, discover opportunity and design a career that works for you.

your future possibilities are the essential skills you will need to have a happy and successful squiggly career.

Spotting the squiggle

Let's start by telling you a bit about us and the light-bulb moment that led to this book. We first met studying Business Management at university, and in June 2013 we got together for a regular catch-up over coffee. We were in a particularly reflective mood that summer's day, sharing our feelings about how life at work had changed since the days of our first jobs.

We both left university ambitious and motivated to climb the career ladder. We had imagined and planned for an end destination that was as far up 'the ladder' as was possible. But the reality of our experiences was somewhat different. Twelve years on, we were both just as ambitious and were enjoying successful careers, but these careers were becoming increasingly unpredictable and somewhat … squiggly.

We had moved organizations, roles and professions much more than we had anticipated. Sarah joked that she had already worked in more companies and roles than her dad had done in his entire career. This gave us pause for thought. We realized that careers weren't really linear anymore; they had become more complicated and complex than that. Every aspect of our working lives seemed to be changing in some way, and the pace of change was speeding up.

Luckily, we were both enjoying and benefitting from these changes. We were learning, exploring new and interesting opportunities, and building relationships with a variety of inspiring and interesting people. But we felt we were in the fortunate minority. Many people we knew were struggling, feeling confused, stressed, anxious and overwhelmed about their careers. Our friends, peers, and people working for us had expressed frustration over their progress, saying things like 'I don't know where I'm going', 'I feel stuck', 'how do I find out what I'm good at?' and 'how do I find a job I love?'

As we sat drinking our coffee, we reflected on this new idea that work was squigglier than it used to be. Sarah picked up a pen and started scribbling on her napkin:

CAREERS IN PAST   CAREERS TODAY

In drawing this sketch, the 'squiggly career' was born. We realized that the career ladder was gone and in its place was the squiggly career. We asked ourselves, wouldn't it be amazing if everyone had the skills they need to succeed in a squiggly career? And decided we wanted to take action to make this happen.

There and then, we started a side project together called Amazing If, to help people be happy and fulfilled at work. Very much accidental entrepreneurs, we were fuelled by an ambition to create a new approach to professional development.

Scaling the squiggle

In the years that followed, our side project took on a life of its own. We began running small skills workshops where people would try out the tools we had designed to support their career development.

At the start of every workshop we drew the staircase and squiggle diagram and shared our hypothesis about how the shape of careers was changing (more on that in the next chapter). Met with nods of agreement every time we showed this sketch, we knew we were onto something. Over the next six years, we ran courses for bigger audiences and tweaked our tools to make them as impactful as possible. The tools became a fundamental part of our own career development as we progressed in leadership roles, navigated parenthood, redundancies and many other personal and professional changes. And as our day jobs grew in size and scale so did our side project.

We worked with organizations large and small to support their employees' career development and we launched the *Squiggly Careers* podcast so we could share our ideas with people who couldn't come to our events. Before we knew it, we had trained thousands of people and developed a large community of advocates and ambassadors of the squiggly career. Hundreds of 'Amazing If Alumni' shared their success stories with us, from being promoted to improving a relationship with a manager to discovering a whole new career. Our small side project had become something much more significant than we'd ever imagined.

Cue this book! For the first time, we have compiled all our ideas, actions, tools and techniques into one place. By reading and working through this book you'll discover new insights into yourself and your career. And before we begin transforming your career, here are some tips on how to make the most of *The Squiggly Career*.

How to use this book

This is a practical book jam-packed full of exercises, tools and techniques. Everything we share is designed to help you discover insights about yourself and take action today, next week and for the rest of your career.

We begin the book in Chapter One by delving deeper into what we mean by the squiggly career and discuss how the career ladder analogy has lost its usefulness in the context of work today.

We hope this book will be your career companion full of scribbles, ideas and successes.

In Chapters Two to Six we focus on the five core skills we have already identified, which will be key to the development of your successful squiggly career:

1. Super Strengths
2. Values
3. Confidence
4. Networks
5. Future Possibilities

Turn the insights you discover into action at work.

Each chapter begins with a brief explanation of what we mean by each skill and explores why it matters in the context of a squiggly career. We then move on to how you can develop each skill and turn the insights you discover into action at work. In some of these chapters we include our own career stories to illustrate how these skills have helped us to learn and succeed in the workplace. You'll find these personal stories in break-out boxes with our names next to them. We finish every chapter with a ten-point summary of the key areas covered.

In Chapter Seven we will address the most common career conundrums including:

1. Should I start a side project?
2. How do I find a mentor?
3. What do I do if my organization doesn't invest in training?
4. How do I achieve work/life balance?
5. Should I stay or should I go?
6. How do I build my personal brand?
7. How do I demonstrate I'm a leader when I don't have a team?

These are the questions we get asked most frequently by people in our workshops and podcast listeners. They are common concerns that become relevant to many of us over the course of our careers. In this chapter, we will share ideas and actions to help you tackle these tricky topics and finish each conundrum with a list of useful resources for you to read, watch or listen to.

In the final chapter, you will find 100 pieces of career advice from people we have worked with or who have inspired us in our careers. Each person has shared their advice with us specifically for this book, so we hope you find their wisdom as invaluable as we have. You'll find nuggets of advice from people like Adam Grant, Professor at Wharton University and author of *Give and Take*, *Originals* and *Option B*, Emma Gannon, author of *The Multi-Hyphen Method* and host of the *Ctrl Alt Delete* podcast, and Carolyn McCall DBE, the CEO of ITV.

Things to keep in mind as you make your way through the book

Get scribbling. There are tools and exercises for you to complete in each chapter, and this book is designed to be written in. If you need more space or want to start an exercise again there are some blank pages at the end of the book. If you're reading this as an eBook, you might want to keep a notebook to hand and use the highlighting function from time to time. We want this to be the most dog-eared book on your shelf, full of turned-down pages and notes – so scribble away!

Adapt the exercises to work for you. Over the past six years we have developed these exercises with the help of our workshop participants but don't be afraid to adapt them to suit your needs. They are not set in stone. If you can spot ways to tweak them so they work even better for you, go for it. This book is your career toolkit to use and personalize to suit you and your needs.

Come back to the exercises more than once. This is really important. These skills are not something you think about developing once, tick off your to-do list then never return to again. View all the exercises as a step towards working out an answer rather than immediately providing the definitive answer. Keep coming back to them and you'll learn new things each time. We have both done the exercises in this book hundreds of times over several years and we continue to find them useful and insightful every time.

Read and re-read. If you have the time, we would suggest reading the book in the order we've written it. Though each chapter can be read in isolation, we think most of you will find it helpful to build on the learning and insights from the previous chapter. After you've read the book once, it's highly likely you'll come back to specific sections to repeat exercises that feel relevant to you at that particular moment in your career.

Get in touch. We'd love to know what you make of our exercises and tools – we want to hear what works and, just as importantly, what doesn't work for you. And if you have ideas for areas you'd like us to cover in the future, please get in touch.

You can find us in a few places:

Instagram: @amazingif
We share daily career tips on Instagram Stories and explore the ins and outs of squiggly careers with our community.

Podcast: *Squiggly Careers* is available for free across all platforms
We host a weekly podcast covering every career topic you can think of, from asking for a pay rise to managing stress at work to how to build your gravitas.

Email: helenandsarah@amazingif.com
If you have any feedback or questions, send us an email. Our favourite part of running workshops is hearing people's success stories afterwards, so we'd love to hear how the book has helped you in your career.

Website: www.amazingif.com
This is where you'll find lots of free career resources, like the ones found in this book, and access to our online courses.

A final word from us

We want to equip you with the ideas, tools and actions to take control of your own career development.

By choosing to read this book you are already taking action to learn and improve, and that's half the battle! Adopting an open mindset, practising self-awareness and prioritizing learning are fundamental to achieving success and finding fulfilment in a squiggly career.

By the end of this book, you'll have gained the insight and confidence to kick-start your squiggly career success. Working through the book will require you to think deeply and reflect thoughtfully on your current and future career but it's also designed to be a fun process. We hope you enjoy reading *The Squiggly Career* and that it supports the careers of you, your colleagues and your friends for many years to come.

Get stuck in and good luck!

Helen and Sarah

Chapter 1
The Squiggly Career

Careers used to be about climbing a ladder; they were predictable, linear and we knew what was coming next. Now everything feels much more uncertain. We all know what it's like to feel overwhelmed and stressed in our jobs, and we're looking for more freedom and fulfilment from the time we spend at work. We came up with the idea of the squiggly career as a way of describing our new reality. All careers today are squiggly, which is why it has never been more important to prioritize your own development and design a career that works for you.

There are many reasons why we face squiggly careers. The last decade has seen seismic shifts in the who, what, where, when and why of work, and created a dramatically different working environment. Before we dive into the five skills you need in order to thrive today, we're going to explore some of the biggest changes of the last decade and what it means for your career today. The who, what, where, when and why of work are all changing. Let's explore each of these and why they matter to you.

WHO we work with

Five generations working side by side

Right now, there are potentially five generations of people working side by side, as an aging population has introduced more demographic diversity into the workplace. Each generation and individual is at a different stage in their career, with varying needs and expectations. A 'one size fits all' approach to career development has become redundant and been replaced by the need for a more personalized framework that recognizes that everyone has different motivations in their career.

Who is at work today?

People aged 75+. Sometimes referred to as 'the traditionalists', this group of people are choosing to work past retirement age thanks to improved health, technology and flexibility.

People aged 55–74. This group of 'baby boomers' have probably experienced a more linear career but now have the opportunity to learn new skills and even retrain for new career options later in life.

People aged 44–54. Typically, this generation is referred to as 'Gen X', and they are identified as being well educated (60 per cent have achieved further education[1]) and having experienced the 'work hard/play hard' approach to careers.

People aged 25–43. This group will represent 75 per cent of the workforce by 2020.[2] For 'Gen Y', finding purpose in their work is important. A tech-savvy group who feel comfortable job-hopping.

People aged under 25. Digital from day one. 'Gen Z' are the most politically and socially active group in work today.

What this means for you: *own your development*

Career paths are disappearing

A more diverse workforce has two significant
implications for your career. The first is the
increasing expectation and need for individuals to
take active ownership of their career development.
Organizations used to do a lot of the hard work
for us, mapping out things like career paths and
promotion plans. Organizations once told us what
to do and where to go, but now we need to be able
to answer those questions for ourselves.

No one cares about your career as much as you do.

Enjoy the journey, it's a long one!

Secondly, we are living and working for longer,
spending an average of 90,000 hours at work in
our lifetime.[3] If you're thirty now, you will
probably continue to work in some capacity
for the next forty years. While this might feel
like a slightly terrifying thought at times, it's
a useful reminder of just how important it is
to design a career that delivers personal
fulfilment, growth and happiness.

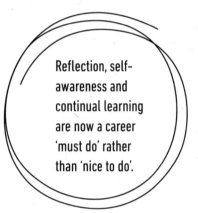

Reflection, self-awareness and continual learning are now a career 'must do' rather than 'nice to do'.

WHAT we work on

The impact of automation

The type of work we're doing has changed. Very few of us have jobs
where we do the same thing day in, day out. This has been primarily
driven by the impact of technology, which is replacing the need for
humans to complete many repetitive and predictable tasks. A McKinsey
report suggests that as technology continues to develop, up to 375 million
workers may need to change their occupational category by 2030.[4]

No two days are the same

Work is now more project based and job specifications become out of date
almost the moment we start a new job, as we adapt to meet the needs of

our organizations. The acronym VUCA – volatile, uncertain, complex, ambiguous – is sometimes used to describe the environment we're now working in, and it doesn't feel like the pace of change is about to slow down. Change asks a lot of people. In a constantly shifting work environment we have to learn new skills, build relationships, communicate effectively and adapt to ongoing shifts in our day-to-day role and responsibilities.

Change is constant

'In order to keep up with the world of 2050 . . . you will above all need to reinvent yourself again and again.'

YUVAL HARARI,
21 LESSONS FOR
THE 21ST CENTURY

Responding and adapting to change also requires organizations to create agile operating structures and develop nimble teams. This means less hierarchy and more restructuring. A 2019 Global Human Capital Trends report by Deloitte discovered that nine out of ten leaders set restructuring as a top priority.[5] This environment means that organizations are looking to hire people who are resilient, adaptable, curious and can demonstrate their ability to learn quickly and succeed in a fast-moving world.

What this means for you: *become a 'learn-it-all'*

Work in progress

As the type of work we do is transforming, our perspective and relationship with learning needs to change too. Learning has to become part of how we work every day, rather than being limited to an occasional training day or team meeting. We need to acknowledge and embrace a 'work in progress' mindset towards our careers, appreciating that there is no point at which we will be 'done' with our professional development.

Lifelong learning

Professor Carol Dweck's research on learning and intelligence proves that our mindset impacts our level of achievement. In a fixed mindset we believe our qualities to be unchangeable, and therefore focus on proving that we are right rather than learning from mistakes. If we adopt a growth mindset we invest energy in stretching our abilities and view failure as an opportunity to learn. The mindset we choose has an enormous impact on how we approach problems and perceive achievement and success. With a fixed mindset we see problems that we aren't smart enough to solve, whereas in a growth mindset we believe we will find a solution, we just haven't got there yet. In her popular TED Talk Dweck refers to this as 'the power of yet'.

Dweck's ideas, which she put forward in a book called *Mindset*, are beginning to be adopted by progressive organizations which recognize the value of integrating learning into their DNA. Satya Nadella, CEO of Microsoft, believes that everyone, including himself, should focus on being a 'learn-it-all' rather than a 'know-it-all'.

> 'You need new ideas and you need new capabilities, but the only way you're going to get those new ideas and new capabilities is if you have a culture that allows you to grow those.'
>
> **SATYA NADELLA, CEO, MICROSOFT**

WHERE and WHEN we work

No more 'nine to five'

Typically, the 'when' of work used to be 9 a.m. to 5 p.m., but according to a YouGov survey in 2018 only 6 per cent of the people surveyed were working the schedule that we traditionally associate with making a living.[6] Employers and employees are beginning to recognize the mutual benefit of individuals defining their own pattern and place of work.

> We are motivated by the freedom to work in a way that suits us best and in return organizations benefit from more productive and diverse employees.

Flexibility is more than working from home

Almost half the people surveyed by YouGov worked flexibly in some way, through initiatives such as job sharing, compressed hours or the four-day week. This is a good example of where flexible working benefits organizations as well as individuals, as 72 per cent of businesses featured in the study reported an increase in productivity as a direct result of implementing flexibility at work in some way.[7]

Where we work

Our 'where' is no longer restricted to the corporate office. Advancement and mass adoption of technology means that an increasing number of people can work anywhere, whether that's at home, in a local coffee shop or a co-working office. The global success of WeWork, a US company that provides shared workspaces for start-ups, freelancers and increasingly for global organizations was established in response to the changing nature of where we work. In 2019 WeWork reported having more than 250,000 members across seventy-two cities and has been valued at US$20 billion.[8]

The 'always on' culture

Today, we have the technology to make working wherever and whenever we want easy. Online collaboration tools such as Microsoft Teams, Slack and Facebook Workplace mean that teams can stay in touch with each other and collaborate regardless of location. However, having such easy access to technology has given rise to an 'always on' culture where it is becoming harder to switch off when we stop working. Many people feel the pressure to be constantly checking their emails and responding to messages, even late at night, at the weekend or on holiday. In fact, seven in ten people say that 'leavism' (people working during their holiday) has occurred in their organization in the last year.[9] Analysis by the UK's Trades Union Congress suggests that in Britain there has been a 15 per cent rise in excessive working hours – defined as people working more than forty-eight hours a week – since 2010.[10]

Loneliness at work

Another challenge with a wide variety of working patterns is the risk of people feeling more isolated and less connected to their colleagues at work. If everyone hot-desks there is no longer the daily 'how's it going?' conversation with your desk neighbour. If you're working at home you miss out on the informal chats that happen when you grab a cup of tea in the office kitchen. And this stuff really matters. An eighty-year study at Harvard tracking health and well-being discovered that how happy we are in our relationships, both at home and at work, has a powerful influence on our health and is the best predictor of long-term happiness.[11]

What this means for you: *design your operating system*

Control the controllable

Identifying what is 'controllable' and what isn't will have a big impact on your ability to define where and when you work. You may be in an organization where the idea of determining the best way of working for you feels like a far-off reality. If this applies to you, identify what you can control and what you can't, and then focus on the former. You might not be in a position to change HR policy, but you could volunteer to champion a hot-desking trial in your team and share the results with other departments. Culture is 'how we do things around here' and comes from all of the people who work together in one place. Start small, try things out individually and within your team, and you might be surprised by how much impact you can have on the whole organization.

Creating time and space to switch off

Technology exists to make your work and life easier and better, though sometimes it can feel like the other way around! You need to take control of how you choose to use technology when you work, as it should help rather than hinder your career. You need to define your own rules and boundaries within which you manage your work and create time and space to switch off (as this will make your work better as well). In his bestselling book *The Joy of Work*, Bruce Daisley suggests a number of practical solutions you could try out, from turning off your notifications or having a digital sabbatical to banning phones from meetings.

Design your own operating system so that technology makes your work life better and easier. Work in a way that works for you (and your organization).

We are all different, and when and where we do our best work changes from person to person. You might not know what your ideal work pattern looks like just yet, but you'll be encouraged to reflect on this further throughout the course of the book. Once you have a clearer view of what works for you, you can then be specific about the changes you need to make. This rarely means making a radical overhaul overnight; for most of us it's about identifying a number of small steps that improve the chances of doing our best work and enjoying the experience along the way.

WHY we work

. Finding fulfilment

Work has evolved from primarily being a source of income to an important part of our personal identity. 'Where do you work?' and 'What job do you do?' are some of the first questions we get asked when meeting someone new. And our reply is normally taken to be a reflection of who we are and what we care about. In his book *How to Find Fulfilling Work*, the philosopher Roman Krznaric says that these days individuals 'want something more: to make a positive contribution to people and planet, and to put their values into practice'. Research conducted by LinkedIn backs up this sentiment, as a study they did with Imperative, a software company focused on employee engagement, revealed that 48 per cent of Baby Boomers and 30 per cent of Millennials (also referred to as Generation Y) would prioritize purpose over pay and job titles.[12] Perhaps, then, a more insightful question to ask when we meet people would be: 'Why do you go to work?'

What this means for you: *discover your 'why'*

Work that energizes and motivates you

'Purpose' has perhaps become an overused and misunderstood word when it comes to careers. A lot of people today feel pressured to have a job that is 'doing good' in some way. Figuring out your why at work doesn't have to mean saving the planet (although if it does then thank you in advance). Instead, focus on discovering what kind of work you are most energized and motivated by – the upcoming exercises in this book will help you identify your why, in particular Chapter Three on values and Chapter Six on future possibilities. These insights will help you make better decisions in your career and balance what's most important to you against the distracting allure of attractive things like a great salary, a swanky office or a grand job title.

A new era of work

We would guess that everyone reading this book will recognize, and have experience of, at least a few of the changes to the who, what, where, when and why of work we have described in this chapter. These shifts are all contributing to a significant change in our careers. There is little point in inflexible career plans when we don't know what jobs will exist in ten years' time, and there's an imperative to find fulfilment in your work if you know you won't be retiring any time soon. Careers are only going to get squigglier, and while our organizations and managers are there to support and guide us, only you can develop the skills you need to succeed at work.

Avoid the knots, embrace the squiggle

Squiggly careers are full of opportunity, but they can also be overwhelming if you don't know what you want to do or where you want to go. This book will help you understand what is important to you, and encourage you to design a career that is fulfilling, enjoyable and as unique as you are. Squiggly careers can be challenging and there will be times when your career might feel more knotty than it does squiggly – but that's where we come in! We have written this book to support you through the tough times, the OK times and the brilliant times. Continually learning and growing is what will help you succeed throughout your squiggly career. If you invest the time, energy and effort in your own development, we promise it will be worth it!

The squiggly career is here to stay, and this book will help you develop the five skills – super strengths, values, confidence, networks and future possibilities – that you need to succeed now, and for the rest of your career.

The Squiggly Career: summary

1 The career ladder analogy has lost its usefulness as a way of describing our ambitions and experience of work.

2 The who, what, where, when and why of work are all changing, simultaneously.

3 It is now possible to be working alongside five different generations of people. A 'one size fits all' approach to career development has become irrelevant and impossible.

4 No one cares about your career as much as you do. Reflection, self-awareness and continual learning are all 'must do' not 'nice to do'.

5 Job specifications become redundant almost the moment you start a new role as everyone is operating in a VUCA (volatile, uncertain, complex and ambiguous) environment.

6 We need to rethink our relationship with learning. Focus on being a 'learn-it-all' rather than a 'know-it-all'.

7 The nine-to-five working day is disappearing. Instead, employers and employees are recognizing the mutual benefit of individuals defining their own patterns and places of work.

8 Design your own 'operating system'. Technology is there to make your work better and easier – make sure the technology you use is working for you, and your organization.

9 Understanding your 'why' at work will improve your decision-making and give you the best opportunity to grow and feel fulfilled.

10 There are five skills that will help you to succeed in a squiggly career: super strengths, values, confidence, networks and future possibilities.

'Whatever money you
might have, self-worth
really lies in finding out
what you do best.'

J. K. ROWLING

Chapter 2
Super Strengths

What are strengths?

Your strengths are the things that you are good at. Your super strengths are the things you're brilliant at. Whether you're an awesome coder or brilliant at building relationships, your strengths are the reason people hire you and how you add value to an organization. The more time you spend using your strengths at work the more impact you will make and the happier you will feel. Gallup, an American performance management company, found that employees who use their strengths are six times more effective and engaged in their role.[13]

How much time have you spent thinking about your strengths recently? In our experience most people have some inkling what their strengths might be, but going a few steps further to identify exactly what they are, and when you use them most, is really valuable. Strengths come from the things you are naturally good at (your natural talents) and the skills and behaviours you have developed through your experiences.

Natural Talents

+

Experiences

=

Strengths

This chapter will help you to both discover and use your strengths frequently and consistently and feel confident sharing them in a way that works for you.

Going from strength to super strength

We all have a wide range of skills, which is just as well, as most jobs require us to be adaptable and employ a number of different abilities and behaviours. What we are particularly interested in are your super strengths. These are the talents that make you really stand out and which you build a reputation for. Think of your super strengths as the positive attributes you would want your colleagues and friends to say about you when you're not in the room.

What about weaknesses?

Spend 80 per cent of your time making your strengths stronger and 20 per cent mitigating specific weaknesses that hold you back in your job.

We all have weaknesses – you, your manager, famous entrepreneurs, CEOs and billionaires, everyone has them. No one is exempt and no one is perfect. But we believe that while it is good to be aware of what your weaknesses may be, you should focus on your strengths. As Peter Drucker, the famous management theorist said, 'You can't build performance on weaknesses. You can build only on strengths.' We recommend spending roughly 80 per cent of your time making your strengths stronger, and 20 per cent of your time improving specific weaknesses that are holding you back from being brilliant in your job. Trying to be good at everything is a thankless and impossible task. You will get more return for your time by focusing on making your strengths stronger than by wasting energy worrying about your weaknesses.

Why super strengths matter in a squiggly career

Discovering and using your strengths will help you in three fundamental ways:

1. Enjoyment at work

If you're thirty today, in all likelihood you have another forty years of work ahead of you, and that's a long time to spend not enjoying your work. And, whatever stage of your career you are at, you have probably spent more time at work this week than with your family and friends. We have to redefine our relationship with work from something to be tolerated – 'work is a necessary evil to be avoided' (Mark Twain) – to something that gives us the chance to make a positive difference and find personal fulfilment. Using our strengths is one way to make this happen, as when we use our strengths in new and different ways research has shown that we experience higher levels of happiness and satisfaction in our work.[14]

2. Attract opportunities

As mentioned in the previous chapter, we are all experiencing more movement in our careers, changing jobs, companies, industries and even type of work more frequently. Knowing what your strengths are will help you explore different career possibilities. You will be able to make brave choices in your career with the knowledge that a role will benefit from the strengths you have to offer. When you start using and sharing your strengths with other people, new and exciting opportunities that you didn't know existed will start finding their way to you.

3. Productive teams

Most of us work as part of a team in some way, shape or form. We are often part of multiple teams simultaneously across different projects within work, and you might also be part of teams outside of your day job through volunteering, side projects or similar activities. Our ability to work together effectively is only going to get more important. A 2019 LinkedIn Global Talent Trends study found that collaboration is one of the top skills in high demand from employers[15] and Gallup research suggests that strengths-focused teams are 12.5 per cent more productive.[16] If you know your strengths, you can actively spot opportunities to use them as much as possible to add value to any team you are part of. And you can do the same for other people by becoming a strengths spotter (see Helen's story later in this chapter) and encouraging everyone to do their best work.

In this chapter, we'll help you to discover your super strengths with a four-step process. We'll then provide lots of ideas for how you can make your strengths show up and stand out. We'll end the chapter with our ten-point summary to remind you of the key points we've covered.

How to discover your strengths: our four-step process

In this section, we'll go through our four-step process to help you discover your strengths. We recommend you repeat the exercises a few times at different times of the day and in different places, as your environment and mood might influence your reflections. For example, you could do a couple of the exercises on your lunch break and try them again in a coffee shop at the weekend. Or you could team up with someone else at work and both complete one exercise a week over the next month and meet weekly to chat through your thoughts.

DISCOVER YOUR STRENGTHS: OUR FOUR-STEP PROCESS

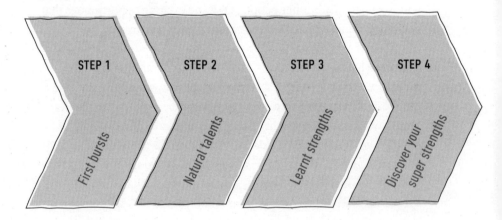

STEP 1 — First bursts

STEP 2 — Natural talents

STEP 3 — Learnt strengths

STEP 4 — Discover your super strengths

Step 1: First bursts

We're going to start with a high-speed strengths exercise. Grab a pen, set a timer to sixty seconds and write down twenty things you are great at.

Hint: if you're running out of ideas don't forget to include things outside of work like hobbies and activities you do with friends and family.

1.   6.   11.   16.

2.   7.   12.   17.

3.   8.   13.   18.

4.   9.   14.   19.

5.   10.   15.   20.

How many did you get? Be reassured, hardly anyone gets twenty on their first go. How did this exercise make you feel? For some people it's uncomfortable to even think about the things they're good at, let alone write them down. So perhaps it felt self-indulgent or even a bit arrogant to list all the things you think you are brilliant at. Or, if you haven't spent much time thinking about your strengths until now, maybe you felt a bit stuck for ideas. This is very common, so don't worry and keep working your way through the exercises.

Next, write down three weaknesses you think you have.

1. ———————————————————————————————

2. ———————————————————————————————

3. ———————————————————————————————

You might have found that easier, which is no surprise as we're often our own biggest critics. However, we're going to turn this on its head – your weaknesses can be really helpful in identifying your strengths. Within each of our weaknesses we can discover an opposing strength. For example, a weakness such as 'lack of attention to detail' can have an opposing strength of 'big-picture thinking', and a weakness of 'not finishing things' can reflect a strength in 'coming up with new ideas'.

Take each of the weaknesses you identified and convert them into an 'opposite' strength below.

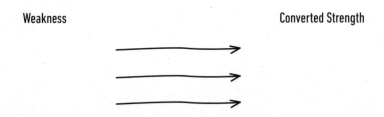

Weakness	Converted Strength

It is worth saying that not all weaknesses have an exact opposite strength so you might need to think laterally. Here are some extra examples which might prove useful if you are struggling to convert your weaknesses.

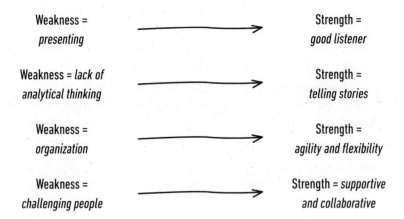

Weakness = presenting	→	Strength = good listener
Weakness = lack of analytical thinking	→	Strength = telling stories
Weakness = organization	→	Strength = agility and flexibility
Weakness = challenging people	→	Strength = supportive and collaborative

Step 2: Natural talents

In this step, we're going to identify your natural talents. These are the things that you are good at without having to be taught. Natural talents are part of our make-up and have been showing themselves, often unconsciously, since we were young; they might include things like being kind or thoughtful, creative or funny. It's likely that you take your natural talents for granted, because they are just part of who you are, so we think of them more as personality traits rather than things that might be useful at work.

To get started, use the space below to write down what you think you naturally do well.

My natural talents: first thoughts

We often find it difficult to spot our natural talents for ourselves. This is why it's helpful to ask people who know you well to share their perspective on what you are good at.

Action: Ask one family member, one friend and one colleague 'What three words would you use to describe me?' Of course, you can ask more, but at a minimum ensure you ask three people who each have a different type of relationship with you.

You can ask people face-to-face, over email or drop them a text or WhatsApp. It's a quick and easy exercise, but our workshop participants often find it revealing. And though we don't explicitly encourage people to say positive words, 99 per cent of the time the words you get back will give you a feel-good boost, which is always nice!

Heads up: this exercise may take you longer to complete than others because it relies on you waiting to hear back from whomever you asked. While you wait for responses you can skip ahead to the next exercise, or wait until you hear back to carry on.

Write down your responses

What three words would you use to describe me?		
Friend:	Family:	Colleague:
1.	1.	1.
2.	2.	2.
3.	3.	3.

Reflect on the words that people use to describe you. Are they the same or different? Of course, you would expect the exact word choice to vary depending on how someone knows you. For example, a friend you play sport with might describe you as 'competitive', whereas a work colleague would be more likely to use the word 'driven'. Where people from different areas of your life have chosen distinctly different words, this could signal an opportunity to bring one of your strengths to light in a different role. For example, if your friends and family describe you as 'thoughtful' but your work colleagues don't see that side of you, this might prompt you to think about whether you could mentor someone at work. You would probably enjoy the process of mentoring and the mentee would benefit from someone who is naturally empathetic and likely to be a good listener.

To build on this exercise you can also ask people for a short explanation of why they selected particular words. This will give you an insight into the stories people tell about you, and when they think you are at your best.

Here's what Sarah found out when she did the exercise:

Sarah's family: mum
Three words: determined, curious, competitive
'I remember when you were thirteen, you really hurt your knee playing netball. You gritted your teeth but kept on playing. You loved games on the beach and hunting for crabs with your dad for hours on end. I see a determined and curious character.'

Sarah's friend: Rachel
Three words: independent, confident, creative
'At university you were always the person who was more confident going your own way than everyone else. You knew what you wanted and would create your own opportunities if the right ones weren't there. You were independent but would always help others if you could. You built strong relationships with a few people, rather than lots of relationships with everyone.'

Sarah's work colleague: Matt
Three words: considerate, focused, calm
'Considerate in both senses: you are considerate of others, and your decisions are carefully considered. You are driven and appear to be clear about where you are heading and how to get there. You speak softly which soothes others and are able to emanate a sense of calm regardless of what's happening.'

Compare the words your friends and colleagues gave you to the initial ideas you wrote down about your strengths at the start of this section. Next, have a look through the list of natural talents we've drawn up over the page and see if any of these words leap out at you. This is not an exhaustive list, so use it as a prompt for self-reflection rather than a final list of words to select from.

Achievement	You are always seeking the next thing to do and complete.	Empathy	You are in tune with the people around you.
Activation	You make things happen.	Excellence	You strive to make things the best they can be.
Adaptability	You are quick to respond to new information and situations.	Focus	You can shut out distractions to achieve your goals.
Analytical	You question things to get a complete view.	Inclusiveness	You make sure people don't feel left out.
Attentive	You spot the small things.	Intelligence	You have always been bright and smart.
Belief	You have an inner sense of purpose that guides you.	Learning	You are naturally curious and love to learn.
Charm	You are able to woo others.	Listening	You give people your full attention.
Command	You love to take charge of people and projects.	Numeracy	You are a natural with numbers.
Communication	You enjoy sharing ideas and thoughts with others.	Organizing	You create order and bring things together.
Competition	You're always looking at how you can be the best.	Positivity	You bring positive energy to any situation.
Connection	You naturally build relationships with others.	Problem-solving	You can see your way around challenges.
Context	You are able to see the bigger picture.	Resilience	You are able to bounce back.
Creativity	You love to create new things and ideas.	Responsibility	You are the person people rely on.
Development	You bring out the best in people and the work you do.	Self-awareness	You have strong insight into who you are and how you show up.
Discipline	You create order and stick to your plans.	Strategic	You connect a future aim with the actions needed to get there.
Efficiency	You use your time effectively.	Supportive	You are always there for people.
Engagement	You attract people to you.	Questioning	You always dig deeper to understand things better.

To finish Step 2 of our strengths-discovery process, write down what you think your top six natural talents are.

1. _____   4. _____

2. _____   5. _____

3. _____   6. _____

Helen's Story: Owning My Strengths

Helen's super strengths: Building Relationships, Positive Energy, Developing Others

Starting Amazing If in 2013 gave me the opportunity to keep trying the exercises out on myself.

In January 2018, as I was thinking about what to do next in my career, I decided to have another go at the natural talents exercise we have just shared with you. I thought it would be interesting to ask two people with very contrasting experiences of me: Kaye, my oldest friend, and Mike, who worked for me at Microsoft, where I was employed at the time.

Kaye had seen me grow through the phases of rebellious teenager, diligent student, focused career woman and multitasking mother. She described my strengths as having 'more energy than a kangaroo' and being 'super bendy', giving the example of when I helped her with a wedding crisis despite being in the middle of a frantic day at work.

Mike, who had seen me in a very different context and over a shorter time period, described me as being 'like Tigger, [you] enter a room with boundless energy and positivity, leaving everybody feeling better for having spent time with you'.

When I looked at their responses side by side I was struck by how similar they were. They had both emphasized the impact my energy had on them. To them I was Tigger and a kangaroo!

This gave me pause for thought. I hadn't really considered my energy to be a strength before. It was just me being me. I'd actually tried to quash this aspect of myself at work as I thought it made me seem less 'professional' and 'serious' as a leader.

I realized I had been dismissing something that gave me the ability to add valuable impact to any role I performed and organization I worked for – my energy. The feedback from Kaye and Mike, and my subsequent reflections, made me realize that I should take ownership of this strength and use it more consciously in my identity at work.

Since then, I have stopped being embarrassed by, or trying to subdue, my natural energy and instead have opted to embrace the opportunities it offers me. And after identifying this as one of my super strengths I've now realized that all my happiest and most successful moments in any given week at work are when I'm able to use my positive energy to make a difference, whether it's to a person, project or meeting.

Knowing this about myself gave me the confidence to make the leap from working at Microsoft to running our venture, Amazing If, full-time. I have spent the last eighteen months bringing all my energy to growing our business – and so far, it's paying off, for both me and Amazing If.

Step 3: Learnt strengths

Just as there are things we are good at without trying, there are things we become good at through learning, effort and practice in our jobs. These are the strengths that you have developed as a direct result of the work you have done in your career so far, for example: procurement expertise, accounting, software knowledge, crisis management or graphic design.

A good place to start reflecting on your learnt strengths is to think about what you do and how you do it. The what includes all the industry (e.g. retail, banking, consumer goods) and professional (e.g. marketing, HR, finance) expertise you have built in your career so far. Imagine someone was applying for your current role – what would they need to know to do your job well? The how should cover the behaviours you bring to work every day, which tend to be more transferable across different industries and professions, and might include things like curiosity, organization, empathy and active listening.

Action: Use the space below to list your whats and hows.

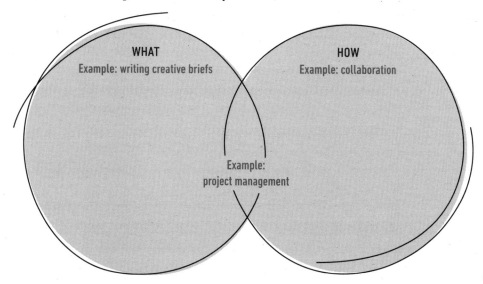

WHAT
Example: writing creative briefs

HOW
Example: collaboration

Example:
project management

Tips for completing the learnt strengths exercise

○ **Include all your jobs.** Dig out your CV and LinkedIn profile to remind
yourself of all the different whats and hows you've gained over your
career so far. You probably have some that you're not using in your
current role, so make sure you don't forget them just because you're
not using them at present. This is a good exercise to do over a
number of weeks so you can add more to the list when you've had
time to reflect.

○ **Be specific.** Break down each of your whats and hows into the most
specific descriptions you can. So rather than writing 'technology
expertise' as a what, be specific about what types of technology
you have expertise in, such as JavaScript, Ruby on Rails, HTML, etc.
Rather than writing 'communication' as a how, think about what
kind of communication you are great at – perhaps it is inspiring people
through presentations, or your ability to influence others through
written communication. Of course, you might be good at multiple
forms of communication, in which case make sure you list these
separately to give yourself credit for all the different ways in which
you add value.

○ **Is it a WHAT or a HOW?** In some cases, you might not be sure if a strength is a what or a how; the point of this exercise is to help you recognize and reflect on all of your many strengths, so don't get caught up in the categorization. If you think you have a strength that is both a what and a how then simply write it sitting between the two circles, where we've added 'project management' on the example on the previous page, as this is an area that can be both a what and a how. You might have a project management qualification or expertise in a particular technique such as managing Agile projects (these are whats), and also be good at organization and bringing together diverse teams (these are hows).

Keep asking yourself why you are good at a particular what or how, and this will help you come up with a longer list. For example: *Why are you good at project management?* Answer: *Stakeholder management, budget management, spot opportunities and risks, dependency planning.* Suddenly you have gone from one strength to five.

○ **Don't try to balance your lists.** There is no correct number of whats or hows, and the two lists don't need to match. Depending on your role and how much experience you have in your career so far you might have lots of whats and not many hows, or vice versa, or your list might be relatively balanced – any combination is fine.

Step 4: Discover your super strengths

So far, we've explored your natural talents and learnt strengths. In this final exercise, we're going to use all of the insights you've discovered about what you're good at, to determine your super strengths. As a reminder, if your strengths are what you're good at, your super strengths are what you're brilliant at.

> You choose your super strengths. You are in control of what you want to be known for and excel in.

From the exercises so far, you should have a long list of strengths and it's likely that your super strengths are already somewhere in that list. The next exercise gives you a useful framework to start making your super strength selections. There are four things to consider that will help you to determine the difference between a strength and a super strength: success, frequency, openness and happiness.

Action: Choose six strengths from all the exercises you have completed so far in this chapter. Pick the strengths you feel most confident about and would like to explore further. Using the table overleaf write down each strength and then score them out of ten (ten being the highest) for each of the four criteria.

Questions to consider as you complete your scoring

Before you get started, take a few minutes to review the descriptions of each criteria and reflect on the questions below.

Success When you use your super strengths, you will have a positive impact at work. You will be able to add more value, and this will show up in both the volume and scale of success you have in your role. You will have lots of examples, big and small, of how you are succeeding in any role where you are using your super strengths.

- Can I share two examples in the last six months where this strength has helped me to be successful?
- Has this strength contributed to the most successful moments in my career so far?

Frequency Your aim is to use your super strengths as often as possible at work. Ideally, you use at least one of your super strengths every day.

- How many times have I used this strength this week?
- Have I used this strength in previous roles as well as in my current job?

Openness This is how visible your strengths are to other people. You want as many people to know what your strengths are as possible and to be open with people about how these strengths inform your work, as these are the talents and skills you will build your reputation around.

- If I asked people, both inside and outside of work, what they thought I was great at, would they say this strength?

○ Review your LinkedIn profile and ask yourself: 'Does my profile help people to spot my strengths?' Your strengths might show up in your summary section, details about the jobs you've completed or recommendations from other people that appear on your page – ideally all three! And if you don't have a LinkedIn profile, make sure you create one. The platform is useful for more than just job searches as it allows you to share your work and stay connected with people you meet but don't work with regularly.

Happiness Not everything we are good at makes us happy. It is important to reiterate that you are choosing your super strengths, they are not being chosen for you. Your super strengths are you at your best, feeling fulfilled and engaged at work, and this should be reflected in how happy they make you feel.

○ When you use this strength does work feel like something you look forward to and get excited about?

○ Does using this strength give you energy?

Super strength selection

	Success	Frequency	Openness	Happiness	Total score / 40
Strengths	On a scale of 1 to 10, how successful have you been using this strength?	On a scale of 1 to 10, how often do you use this strength?	On a scale of 1 to 10, how visible is this strength to other people?	On a scale of 1 to 10, how happy do you feel when using this strength?	
1.					
2.					
3.					
4.					
5.					
6.					

Interpreting your results

In this exercise it's not as simple as assuming that your highest scores equal your super strengths. Before you can reach any conclusions, you need to delve a bit deeper into your results.

Start by looking at the strengths with the highest scores for happiness. All the other dimensions of a super strength (success, frequency and visibility) can be developed, but if a strength doesn't make you happy, then you don't want it to be a super strength. For example, perhaps you have organization as a strength. It's something you've had some success with, you use it frequently in your job and other people would say you were good at it, but it saps your energy and isn't something you love doing. You might be good at it, but you're never going to enjoy it enough to put in the effort required to become brilliant at it. It's never going to be your super strength.

Super strengths action plan

Once you've identified the strengths that make you happy, you're going to take action to turn these strengths into super strengths. As an example, look at the scores below for two strengths: project management and creative thinking.

Strength	Success	Frequency	Openness	Happiness	Total score /40
Project management	5	5	6	9	25
Creative thinking	7	4	4	9	24

In this example, you have a strength, project management, that makes you very happy, but you have lower scores in your success, frequency and openness. Success is often a natural outcome of doing something that makes you happy, and doing it frequently and visibly, so prioritize looking at how you can use your strength more (frequency) and how you can ensure other people know what a great job you're doing (openness).

Here are some examples of the type of actions that could be taken to increase the scores in each of the four criteria, helping turn them from strengths into super strengths.

Strength	Increase Success	Increase Frequency	Increase Openness	Increase Happiness
Project management	1. Ask the people you frequently work with for one idea on how you could use your project management skills to support the team in delivering your collective objectives. 2. Ask your manager for feedback on how your project management skills could increase your impact.	1. Identify one problem your organization needs to solve that could benefit from your project management skills. 2. Volunteer to mentor a colleague who would like to improve their project management skills.	1. Update your LinkedIn profile so that your summary includes reference to your project management skills and how you use them to add value in a role. 2. Run a monthly session on the 'brilliant basics' of project management that anyone in your organization can attend.	1. Join a network of people who share the same passion for project management as you (this could involve virtual or physical meet-ups). 2. Identify two learning objectives that will further build your expertise in this area – what are you going to read, watch and listen to that will inspire and challenge you?
Creative thinking	1. Set objectives to define how you will know whether you've been successful in using this strength in the next week, month and six months; make a plan to support your delivery on those objectives.	1. Find an internal project that would benefit from creative thinking and offer to run a skills workshop or 'lunch and learn' session for the team. 2. Identify a volunteering or side-project opportunity where you can specifically offer your creative thinking skills.	1. Talk to your manager about how your strength could be useful within the team. 2. Write a blog post sharing your insights about how to apply creative thinking at work.	1. Identify three creative thinkers outside of your industry or area of expertise and see what you can learn from their approach.

You're now on your way to turning your chosen strengths into super strengths. Take a moment to write your newly identified super strengths in the space below and reflect on them.

_____

Are you in the right job?

It is worth considering that if you identify a strength that you want to be known for and you can't see a way to increase the frequency of use in your current job, you may not be in the right job. There are always actions you can take to improve how you use your strengths in your current role, but if the job you are in doesn't need your super strength then it might be a case of a square peg in a round hole. Recognizing this does not mean you have to take immediate action to change your job, but it does mean it is time to start thinking about different roles that will benefit much more from the value you bring to them.

Now that you have an idea what your super strengths are, you need to make sure they show up and stand out as much as possible. The final section of this chapter focuses on ideas for practical actions that you can implement straight away to apply your strengths in as many ways as possible.

Make your strengths show up and stand out

Strengths-based feedback

This is a simple, straightforward and powerful way to get insight into whether the strengths you are using are having a positive impact. Get into the habit of regularly asking the people you work with, 'Can you tell me when you think I'm at my best?'

'Can you tell me when you think I'm at my best?'

If you want to make it even more specific you could ask something like: 'Can you tell me where you think I add most value in this project?' or 'What examples did you see of me at my best this month?' You can ask anyone for strengths-based feedback and you don't need to combine this with asking for ideas on how to improve at the same time (if you'd like to read more about receiving feedback we cover this in part two of Chapter Six: Future Possibilities).

Super strengths speed dating

This is an exercise we sometimes run in workshops and works well with a group of six or more people. Everyone gets on their feet and finds a partner. You share a strength and talk about one way you use it in your job today and one idea for how you can use it more. The other person then reciprocates. Then you move on to a new partner and repeat the exercise, sharing the same strength but this time talking about a new idea. This has two benefits: it gives you practice in feeling confident sharing your strengths out loud and encourages you to come up with new ideas for how to use a strength more in your current role.

One tip for this exercise is to ban the use of 'diminishing words', such as 'I'm *quite* good', or 'I *think* I'm good at' or '*Other people* tell me I'm good at'. The first round might feel awkward, but by the third or fourth go everyone has grown comfortable with it. We often end the exercise with everyone sharing their super strength with the group. Initially people expect to find this a bit embarrassing, but we find that participants enjoy sharing how they make a positive contribution at work and this has the added bonus of encouraging everyone to appreciate each other's strengths too.

Job crafting

When was the last time you looked at your job specification? For most people it was when they applied for a job. It is not surprising that we are not constantly referencing our job specifications, as the majority of roles require us to be flexible about exactly what we spend our time doing day to day. This affords you, the employee, the opportunity to do something called job crafting. This refers to the act of moulding your job around you and your strengths, alongside what the organization needs you to deliver. Your manager is a critical part of the job crafting process, as you can't do this alone. If you

> Job crafting is not a wish list of doing all the good stuff and ditching the boring bits. Your focus is on both what's best for you and for your team.

spot an opportunity to evolve your role to better suit your strengths, the first thing we would recommend is sharing your strengths with your manager and discussing your ideas for how you could add more value to the team.

It's worth bearing in mind that job crafting is rarely a one-meeting process. It often takes time to alter a role, as the changes might impact other people, or you might need to wait for the right project to come along.

Side projects/volunteering

Look out for opportunities to develop your strengths outside of your day job. Of course, the ultimate objective is to maximize your value in your day job, and you don't have to start a side project from scratch, but volunteering your time to another team within work, or a group outside of work, can provide you with an opportunity to develop your strengths in new contexts, make them more visible and learn from other people (see side projects in Chapter Seven: Squiggly Career Conundrums, to read more about this).

Social media

Make sure your strengths are visible everywhere that you are. They should be clear in your LinkedIn summary statement and any other social media you use for work too. Think about how your strengths show up in your online interactions, when you're commenting on posts or sharing content that interests you. What would happen if a future employer Googled you? Can they work out what your strengths are from a couple of clicks?

Super Strengths: summary

1 Strengths are the things you are good at, super strengths are the things you are brilliant at.

2 Spend 80 per cent of your time focused on making your strengths stronger and 20 per cent of your time mitigating any specific weaknesses relevant to your job.

3 Your strengths are a combination of your natural talents and your learnt experience.

4 Natural talents are the things that you are good at without being taught. We often take these talents for granted and underestimate their positive impact at work.

5 Ask a family member, friend and work colleague for three words to describe you. Other people can often see our impact more clearly than we can ourselves.

6 Your learnt strengths are a combination of your whats (the knowledge and expertise you have in your industry and profession) and your hows (the behaviours you bring to work).

7 You choose your super strengths and can evaluate the difference between a strength and a super strength using four criteria: success, frequency, openness and happiness.

8 Know what you want people to say about you when you are not in the room.

9 Ask for strengths-based feedback: 'Can you tell me when I've been at my best this week?' This will make sure your impact matches your positive intent.

10 Take practical actions to make sure your strengths show up and stand out. This includes: job crafting, side projects, team-based strengths exercises and developing your online profile.

'I have learned that as long as I hold fast to my beliefs and values – and follow my own moral compass – then the only expectations I need to live up to are my own.'

MICHELLE OBAMA

Chapter 3
Values

What are values?

Values are the unique attitudes and beliefs that motivate and drive us. They are what make you 'you', so it might help to think of them as being a bit like your career DNA. They are a fundamental part of who you are, as they reflect what matters to you most. Values can sometimes feel like a vague and abstract concept but there are practical actions you can take to discover your values and apply them in your day-to-day life at work. In this chapter, we're going to show you how.

Why your values matter in a squiggly career

Understanding what your values are and how they connect to your work helps you in three ways:

1. **Be yourself at work**

   You might have heard the phrase 'we want employees to bring their "whole selves" to work'. Essentially this means turning up to work and being yourself, not feeling as though you are putting on an act or trying to be something you're not. This is beneficial for you and your employer, as 'pretending' takes up a lot of energy that could be better applied to doing valuable work. If you are able to live out your values at work and express them openly, you will feel more comfortable and confident as well as being more productive. In the context of careers where we are all working longer and with many more people, inauthenticity will affect the quality of your relationships and happiness at work.

2. Build your empathy

Empathy is your ability to walk in other people's shoes, to understand things from someone else's perspective which might be different to your own. We often do the values exercises in this book with teams of people who work together. The feedback we receive is that people are surprised at how much better they feel they know their colleagues as a result of understanding what each other's values are. When you understand someone you are much more likely to work together collaboratively and constructively, increasing your ability to overcome challenges together that previously might have felt insurmountable.

3. Make better decisions

Over the course of your career you are going to make lots and lots of decisions. Decisions about which projects to work on, which roles to apply for, what industry to work in and even when to switch career. And switching careers is becoming increasingly common, with almost 50 per cent of people considering a career pivot at any given time.[17] This includes perpetual 'pivoter' Amelia Kallman, whose career has seen her transition from being an actress in the US, a burlesque star in China and now a futurist, speaker and author in London. She says of her squiggly career: 'I'm always curious, I enjoy people, and I love to imagine what's possible. Every stage has taught me new lessons about who I am, who I want to be, and the kind of life I want to live.'

Using your values as a decision-making filter means you're less likely to be distracted by what we call 'shiny objects' like salaries, job titles or a swanky office. These things might give you short-term satisfaction but can't compete with the opportunity to live your values at work. Using your values to guide your choices also helps you make the right decision for you and avoid being

Knowing your values will help you make better decisions, based on what motivates and drives you (and not what other people expect or think you should do).

influenced by what other people might expect or think you should do. It's a career cliché to say 'focus on the journey, not the destination', but in our careers today the idea of a destination has disappeared. It doesn't mean we're suggesting you ignore the future (as you'll find out in Chapter Six: Future Possibilities) but we are recommending using your values as a continual career compass to guide your decisions and actions.

How are values formed?

Our values are developed as we move from childhood to early adulthood and there are three specific phases that we all go through and come out of with our values formed. We describe these three stages of our development as spongey, copy-cat and rebel – see the diagram below.

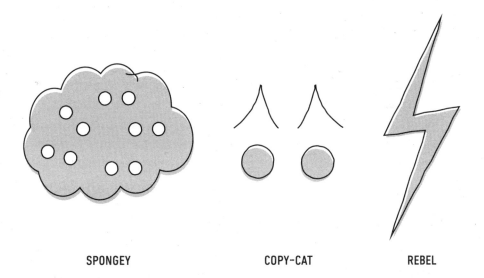

SPONGEY   COPY-CAT   REBEL

The phases of development

Values start forming from the moment we're born and the spongey phase, often referred to as the 'imprint period', lasts until we are around seven years old.[18] In our early years we absorb the world around us and accept what we experience mostly without question. This is when we learn a sense of right and wrong, and as a young child our parents and significant carers are the biggest influence on our behaviour.

We then move into the copy-cat phase or 'modelling period' between eight and thirteen years old. At this point we try on different traits and behaviours, copying and imitating people around us who hold some sort of appeal, such as teachers, siblings and classmates.

As we enter our teenage years, we enter the rebel phase and start to test out different ideas about what we believe and what matters to us. At this point in our lives, we have more choice about who we spend our time with and what we spend our time doing. We tend to become heavily influenced by our friends, peers and more impersonal sources such as the media, especially when our 'tribe' is represented in some way. The rebel phase can result in a period of personal conflict as we may have to challenge some of our earlier-held beliefs about good and bad, right and wrong.

Our values are fully formed by the time we're in our early twenties, and from this point onwards they start to influence our behaviour and happiness. Most people struggle to consciously articulate what their values are. So, if this is a completely new concept to you then don't worry, the majority of people who come to our workshops are in the same boat. In our experience, it takes time to really get to grips with your values. It is worth the effort though, as it's also the area that we see has the most transformational impact with regards to taking control of your own career happiness and success. The exercises in this chapter will give you a toolkit to start discovering your values and, as with all our tools, we hope you will keep coming back to repeat the exercises and add reflections as you start taking action to design a successful squiggly career for yourself.

Guiding principles

There are a few principles that are useful to bear in mind before you begin the values exercises.

1. Core values

We all have a number of principles that are important to us. What we are focusing on in this book is discovering three to five core values.

These are the values that are the most important to you and that, if forced, you would prioritize over other areas that still matter to you.

2. There are no right or wrong values

When you start to reflect on your values it's easy to let judgement creep in. Don't fall into the trap of thinking that some values are good or better than others. A person with fairness as a value is not better or worse than someone who has achievement as a value. There are no 'right' or 'wrong' values. The key to exploring your values is to be honest with yourself about what is most important to you. And if you are doing this exercise with your team at work, remember not to be critical of each other's values either.

3. Values work for and against you

Because your values are such strong internal drivers, they impact your happiness and can make life challenging at times. Let's say that honesty is one of your core values. This could mean you're so honest you inadvertently hurt someone's feelings, or you might find yourself in a situation where you can't be completely honest, which feels frustrating. Understanding how your values can work for and against you helps you to understand the impact you have on other people. Knowing your values doesn't give you an excuse for bad behaviour but it does give you a way to talk about what is important to you and why you are feeling a certain way. Knowing your own and other people's values can break down barriers and build bridges with people.

4. Values for life

You don't have a set of values for work and a set of values for home. You have what makes you 'you' regardless of where you are. In this book, our examples are all set in a work context because our focus is on squiggly careers, but just as behaving in line with your values at work will make you happier in your job, living out your values at home has the same effect. It is particularly

> Career destinations have disappeared. Your values are a continual career compass to guide your decisions and actions.

important to repeat the values exercises in this chapter in various different surroundings because, as you'll read in Sarah's story later in the chapter, this will prompt new insights and accelerate your self-awareness.

5. Values need time

The exercises in this chapter will give you everything you need to start identifying and applying your values today. That said, it is unlikely that you will have it all cracked on your first attempt. It took both of us a few years to fully reflect on and refine our values. Though it may take some time to figure out, you will start to see the positive impact that understanding your values can have straight away.

Understanding your values

Over the next few pages, you'll work through five exercises that will help you build a picture of what your values are.

1. Reflecting
2. Spotting
3. Scanning
4. Prioritizing
5. Defining

Step 1: Reflecting

By looking back on your career experiences so far you will uncover some hints about what it is you value in a job. And this reflection will also help you to create a list of your career must-haves, the things that are essential for you in any job, and must-nots, the things you want to avoid wherever possible. As you'll see in the example opposite, we're going to ask you to plot your career highs and lows so far, making some specific notes about when things were going well and what was happening when you dipped into the unhappy zone.

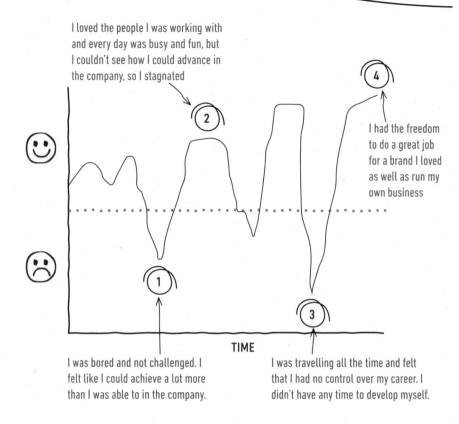

I loved the people I was working with and every day was busy and fun, but I couldn't see how I could advance in the company, so I stagnated

I had the freedom to do a great job for a brand I loved as well as run my own business

TIME

I was bored and not challenged. I felt like I could achieve a lot more than I was able to in the company.

I was travelling all the time and felt that I had no control over my career. I didn't have any time to develop myself.

To start drawing your own career chart, think about your very first job. What were you doing and how did it make you feel? Mark where your feelings were on the scale in the chart on the next page. Write down the different emotions you were feeling in this role and what triggered them. For example, perhaps you were happy because you were in a team with lots of energy and ideas and you had a manager who gave you lots of autonomy. Or perhaps you felt frustrated because you didn't feel that the work you were doing was meaningful, or the pace was too slow.

Now, keep tracking each step of your career up to where you are right now. Think about the different moves, changes and moments that stand out for you. Each time you hit a career high or a career low, take a moment to capture those feelings and insights about what was going on. You'll end up with a line charting your emotions and lots of descriptions, which we can use to look for clues about your values.

TIME

:)

:(

Look at what you have written down in the career high moments. Can you see any consistent words or themes emerging when you've been at your happiest at work? It can also be helpful to repeat this exercise using different timescales. For example, after plotting your whole career to date, why not zoom in and plot the last two years, or focus only on your current role. You could even do it for one week, plotting the highs and lows you have each day. There are some blank pages at the back of the book if you want to repeat several iterations of this exercise.

Action: Review your career graph (or graphs if you have done multiple ones) and use the space below to write down your three career must-haves and three career must-nots.

Career must-haves
☺ E.g. Must have opportunity to learn and grow constantly.

☺

☺

☺

Career must-nots
☹ E.g. Must not be required to travel lots.

☹

☹

☹

This exercise will give you some initial hints as to what your values are. You should start to recognize that you are normally happiest at work when you apply your values, and that periods marked by feelings of frustration or demotivation are often when your values are being challenged or are missing from your working life.

Step 2: Spotting

Asking yourself 'What are my values?' can feel a little daunting, so instead we recommend you start with 'What's important to me?' Answering this question can help you to spot words that turn up repeatedly and clearly hold meaning and importance for you. But before you can answer that question, it's helpful to break down the idea further and think about what is important to you in specific contexts.

What is important to you about:

1. The people you work with?
2. The work that you do?
3. The organizations you work for?
4. The environment you work in?

Answer each question and jot down your initial thoughts in the space below.

What's most important to you about ...	
People	
Work	
Organization	
Environment	

Everyone answers these questions in their own way as our responses draw on our unique beliefs and feelings. For some people it might really matter to work for an organization that has a well-established brand whereas other people love being part of small start-up environments. It is also interesting to reflect on what you wrote down first and how much you wrote for each category. It might be that the work you do is much more important to you than the people, organization or environment. Or you're quite open to different types of work but the people you work with is top of your list of priorities.

Step 3: Scanning

We've started to discover what your values might be. Our next step is to explore a number of words that might be important to you.

Action: Scan through the list below and highlight the words that jump out to you. You're looking for words that feel like you. This is not a full or a final list of values, these are some words to get you started. If you think of other words that matter to you, add them in using the blank spaces at the bottom of the table.

Acceptance	Equality	Justice	Privacy
Achievement	Excellence	Kindness	Progression
Appreciation	Excitement	Knowledge	Purpose
Authority	Focus	Learning	Rationality
Belonging	Freedom	Logic	Reciprocity
Capability	Friendship	Loyalty	Respect for others
Challenge	Fun	Meaning	Responsibility
Choice	Growth	Mindfulness	Routine
Control	Harmony	Modesty	Safety
Courage	Health	Newness	Self-respect
Creativity	Helpfulness	Obedience	Spirituality
Curiosity	Honesty	Openness	Stability
Determination	Honour	Order	Success
Discipline	Inclusion	Partnership	Tolerance
Diversity	Independence	Passion	Variety
Efficiency	Indulgence	Peace	Vision
Energy	Influence	Politeness	Wealth
Enthusiasm	Intelligence	Power	Wisdom
SPACES BELOW FOR YOUR OWN WORDS			

Step 4: Prioritizing

In the last three exercises you have been reflecting on what makes you happy at work, what areas of the work environment are most important to you and which 'value words' most resonate with you. All of this is stimulus for our next exercise, where we are going to prioritize what is most important to you. This will be the activity that helps you to determine your core values from a longer list of things that are important to you.

Action: To do this next exercise you need to go through the insights you have gathered in the first three exercises and create a shortlist of the ten words that you are most drawn to as potential values.

Review everything you have written down and select the ten words that feel most important to you right now. If you've got too many in your list, you might be able to cluster similar words together. For example, if you have a theme of learning and growth and you have also selected the word 'knowledge' from the longlist, you might feel that they are all getting at the same thing. For now, on your shortlist, you could just call this 'learning/growth/knowledge'. You'll come back to these words later, so don't worry too much about getting it 'right' first time.

Write your ten words in the left-hand column of the blank table below.

	Potential values	Your values prioritization
1		
2		
3		
4		
5		
6		
7		
8		
9		
10		

Next, we're going to go through a series of questions which will force you to choose which words are the most important to you, resulting in a prioritized list of your values. Be sure to follow these steps carefully to make sure you get the process right. We've included an example list of values to demonstrate how this works.

Action 1

Consider the first two words in your chart and ask yourself which is more important to you, word number one or word number two? So, in the example we've provided below, you'd be asking which is more important to you, 'freedom' or 'energy'? Depending on your answer, put a tick in the right-hand column by the word you chose.

	Potential values	Your values prioritization
1	Freedom	✓
2	Energy	
3	Growth	
4	Achievement	
5	Optimism	
6	Appreciation	
7	Friendship	
8	Relationships	
9	Openness	
10	Success	

Then, repeat the exercise by asking yourself which is more important, word one or three? In this example that would be 'freedom' or 'growth'. Again mark your answer – so if the answer is 'freedom' again, there will now be two ticks next to it. Keep asking the same question of which word is more important to you, one or four, one or five, and so on until you get to one or ten. By the end, you'll have a list that will look something like the below (if you started with a list of ten words, there should now be nine ticks).

	Potential values	Your values prioritization
1	Freedom	✓ ✓ ✓ ✓ ✓
2	Energy	
3	Growth	
4	Achievement	
5	Optimism	✓
6	Appreciation	
7	Friendship	✓
8	Relationships	✓
9	Openness	
10	Success	✓

Action 2

Now, move on to your second word ('energy' in this example) and start the process again. So this time ask yourself, what is more important to you, word two or three ('energy' or 'growth')? Mark down your answers and then repeat with two or four, two or five, two or six, until you get to the last one, two or ten.

Action 3

Start again with word number three against words four to ten and repeat the process with each of the remaining words in your list until you get to the very last question: which is more important word, word nine or ten?

Once you have completed the whole process, you'll end up with a list that looks a bit like the below. You will have forty-five ticks if you started off with ten words.

	Potential values	Your values prioritization
1	Freedom	✓✓✓✓✓
2	Energy	✓✓✓✓✓
3	Growth	✓✓✓✓✓✓
4	Achievement	✓✓✓✓✓✓✓
5	Optimism	✓✓✓✓✓
6	Appreciation	✓
7	Friendship	✓
8	Relationships	✓✓✓✓✓✓✓
9	Openness	✓✓
10	Success	✓✓✓✓✓✓

This cheat sheet will help you to follow the process if you need a reminder.

What is more important ...?

Word 1	Word 2	Word 3	Word 4	Word 5	Word 6	Word 7	Word 8	Word 9	Word 10
1 or 2									
1 or 3	2 or 3								
1 or 4	2 or 4	3 or 4							
1 or 5	2 or 5	3 or 5	4 or 5						
1 or 6	2 or 6	3 or 6	4 or 6	5 or 6					
1 or 7	2 or 7	3 or 7	4 or 7	5 or 7	6 or 7				
1 or 8	2 or 8	3 or 8	4 or 8	5 or 8	6 or 8	7 or 8			
1 or 9	2 or 9	3 or 9	4 or 9	5 or 9	6 or 9	7 or 9	8 or 9		
1 or 10	2 or 10	3 or 10	4 or 10	5 or 10	6 or 10	7 or 10	8 or 10	9 or 10	

Action 4

Count up your ticks for each word and write the four words with the highest scores below:

Value 1: _____

Value 2: _____

Value 3: _____

Value 4: _____

Hard choices

Before we move on to the final exercise, take a minute to reflect on the process you have just been through. You may have noticed that some of the choices felt harder than others to make and you struggled to make a decision between a couple of values. This dilemma usually occurs when you are choosing between two core values as both things will be really important to you.

Or you may have found it hard to choose between two words because the words mean something very similar to you. Refer back to the previous example, where we had growth, learning and knowledge as separate words on our list of potential values. If you have three words on your list that mean the same thing to you, when you go through the prioritizing exercise this will split your scores: something that could be a core value for you would then end up with a lower score because it is spread across three words that represent the same value for you. If you spot that you have two or three words that mean the same thing to you, join them together using slashes, e.g. growth/learning/knowledge, and then add a new potential value so you have a full list of ten again, and repeat the exercise. You can repeat the exercise as many times as you need to and play around with different words and bringing words together or separating them to see what you find out.

Words with low or no score

It is important to remember that if some of the values on your longlist received low or no scores, it doesn't mean that they aren't important to you. These things still really matter to you as they made it onto your shortlist, they are just not your core values.

Step 5: Defining

Identifying what your values are is incredibly important but it's just as
important to be able to define what you mean by each value. You need to
be able to share what a value means to you, otherwise it's easy for other
people to put their own interpretation on your words. For example,
respect could mean 'people value my knowledge and contribution' to one
person and it could also mean 'there is appreciation for different people's
views and perspectives' to another. Same word, different meanings. Before
you share your values with other people make sure you have interrogated
them for yourself. And then, when you do share your values, make sure to
include both what they are and what they mean to you.

To get started, pick the four values that received the highest score in
the previous exercise and give yourself one minute per value to write
down the best definition you can. Writing a definition can feel daunting so
putting a time limit on it means you get the ball rolling, which is all you
need to do at this stage. You'll be surprised at what you can come up with
in a minute!

Sixty-second value definition challenge

Value 1: _____. I define this as _____

_____

Value 2: _____. I define this as _____

_____

Value 3: _____. I define this as _____

_____

Value 4: _____. I define this as _____

_____

There is another benefit to this definition exercise. Sometimes, in your definition, there may be a word that resonates more strongly with you than the one you started with. For example, if you started with a value of 'freedom', which you defined as 'making unconstrained choices about my life and career', the word 'choice' may be a better fit for you. This is an iterative process and you don't have to get your list perfect straight away. Keep coming back to this exercise and make changes as you continue to reflect.

Practise talking about your values in a way that works for you, as when other people know your values, they can help you live them more.

Sarah's Story: The Value of Values

Sarah's core values: Achievement, Ideas, Learning, Variety

I was sat on level twenty-four of a thirty-one-storey skyscraper in Canary Wharf, the financial district of London, determined to work out my values. My plan was to identify my values between 9 and 10 a.m., tick that off my to-do list and then move on to the rest of my day. I dutifully worked through a values exercise someone had given me and came up with what I thought were my values: achievement, progression, rewards and competition. Done.

At the next catch-up with my manager I proudly shared the process I had been through and the values I had come up with. After a slight pause, she said, 'Are you sure they're your values, they only sound like a bit of you. I think you should take some time to really think about this.' This wasn't the outcome I had expected. To be honest I had been hoping for something along the lines of a verbal 'gold star' for managing to get the activity done in the midst of a really busy time at work.

I wasn't sure what to do next other than to repeat the process. This time I did the same exercise while sitting in a coffee shop in Soho. A couple of lattes later and my values emerged as: learning, curiosity, development and coaching.

I was surprised – between Canary Wharf and Soho I seemed to have morphed into a different person.

I decided I must be doing the exercise wrong. I went back to the person who had shared the process with me to ask her to explain it to me again. She explained that I wasn't doing the exercise incorrectly; rather, I was approaching the concept of 'values' with the wrong mindset. She shared with me that she had been reflecting on her values for over fifteen years. She was confident in four of her core values but was still grappling with whether she had a fifth to add to the list.

That one conversation was a pivotal moment for me as I started to appreciate that personal and professional development wasn't something to be ticked off my to-do list.

I've been working on my values for over eight years now and it's only in the last eighteen months that I've added 'variety' to the three core values I was confident in: achievement, ideas and learning. Reflecting on and understanding my values has impacted every aspect of my career, from encouraging me to make what felt like brave but right decisions – such as asking to work part-time at the same time as being promoted – to simple things like introducing myself using my values when I started a new job.

Acting on your values

To start to work with your values more consciously, it's important to be clear on what actions you can take next. We've outlined three activities that will help you think about, develop and act on your values:

1. Ongoing values reflection
2. Live your values more
3. Understanding other people's values

For each activity, we've given two examples of actions you could take, and then left a space for you to write down what feels like the best next step for you – it might be one of the ideas we've suggested or a new thought you've had.

Ongoing values reflection

Memory test: Set a reminder in your diary for a week's time and see how many of your values you can remember without revisiting your notes from the last exercise. Reflect on what springs to mind and why you remembered or forgot some. Is there one value you are confident in, whereas you are still grappling with the others? Use this as a prompt to repeat the prioritization exercise.

Career clues: Repeat the career must-haves and must-nots exercise on p.54 but this time focus the timescale on a single week in your current job. Reflect at the end of each day and document the highs and lows, thinking about how they align with your potential values.

Your action:

Live your values more

Job crafting: Think about one change you could make to your job today that would help you live one of your values more. Identify how this change would benefit you *and* your organization. For example, if innovation is important to you, could you talk to your manager about trialling using 10 per cent of your time each week to explore new projects?

Choices: The next time you have a decision to make about a new project or opportunity, evaluate your possible options using your values. For each option give each of your values a score out of ten to reflect how well you think a decision aligns with living that value.

Your action:

Understanding other people's values

What's important to you? Choose a project where you're not making as much progress as you would like. Talk to one of your colleagues and ask them what they think is important about that project. See if you can spot their values in how they respond.

Manager: Think about whether there's a way you can share your values with your manager, perhaps as part of a development or review conversation. By sharing your own values or, if it's easier as a starting point, some of the things that are most important to you about work, you might prompt your manager to reciprocate. Or you could suggest to your manager running a team values session, so everyone gets to know each other a bit better.

Your action:

Values discovery

The values discovery process can be transformational. Values are a tricky thing to pin down and not everyone has spent time thinking about them. When we run our workshops, the values section is where we see the most 'aha!' moments – people suddenly see things in a different way and gain a newer and deeper understanding of themselves. Of course, not everyone discovers their values in one workshop, far from it! Feeling confident that you have identified your values and becoming comfortable talking to others about them takes time. However, if you start using some of the tools in this chapter to reflect on what your values might be, you'll be on the right track. There are so many small actions with immediate benefits that you can take to help you feel happier at work. Understanding what your values are and putting them into practice as part of your day-to-day job is an integral part of designing a career that works for you.

Values: summary

1 Values are what make you 'you'. They are the things that motivate and drive you.

2 Your values are formed in three phases – spongey, copy-cat and rebel – and they are fully established by the time you reach your early twenties.

3 Knowing your values helps you in three ways: being yourself at work, using insight and empathy to build stronger relationships, and acting as a career compass to help you make better decisions.

4 You have around three to five core values. These are your strongest motivators, the things that are ultimately the most important to you.

5 You only have one set of values and they impact all aspects of your life both at work and at home. Values aren't up for judgement. No value is better than any other.

6 Your values can work for or against you. Understanding how to use your values positively at work will increase the impact you can have.

7 Knowing your career must-haves and must-nots will give you valuable clues about what your values might be.

8 Defining what your values mean will help you to share them with other people.

9 Understanding other people's values builds teams with strong empathy, high trust and creates an environment where everyone feels comfortable being themselves.

10 Living your values at work is on your to-do list for life. Revisit and review your values and their definitions regularly to see if they still feel right.

'I think any form of
self-expression is half
confidence, half sheer
hard work and, maybe, a
bit of talent thrown in.'

KATE WINSLET

Chapter 4
Confidence

What is confidence?

Confidence is having belief in yourself. It's the ability to recognize your successes, trust in your abilities and be resilient enough to bounce back from bumps in the road. And it's not only about belief in yourself; when you are confident, other people will trust and believe in you too. Confidence is a skill. And the good news about skills is that they can be learnt, practised and improved.

Think of someone whom you would describe as confident; what other words would you use to paint a picture of that person's characteristics? Words such as brave, resilient, authentic, inspiring and calm often spring to mind. While words like arrogant, egocentric and manipulative may also be on the list (and we'll come back to this shortly), most people consider confidence to be a positive attribute, and it is something most of us would like to have more of.

Everyone experiences moments of doubt or situations where they would like to improve their confidence. It is often the case that we perceive particular people as confident because we see them at their best, or perhaps they have dedicated time and energy to feeling and appearing confident in that moment.

Why confidence matters in a squiggly career

Building confidence can help you in your career in three important ways:

1. **Develop resilience**

   In Chapter One: The Squiggly Career, we mentioned the significance of change as a defining characteristic of the careers we are experiencing. Jobs are rapidly appearing and disappearing because of technology and restructuring. Some skills are becoming less relevant as our work evolves and new ones take their place. Expertise is no longer the only career badge of honour; instead, it is the person who can talk about how they have bounced back from challenge, stretched themselves and learnt from their failures, that holds people's interest.

2. **Take action**

   Self-awareness is only the first step of a fulfilling career. It needs to be converted into action and that is not always easy. It could mean making difficult decisions, like changing role or profession. Or it could mean taking a risk, like scaling your side project or applying for a role where you'll be leading a team for the first time. All of these actions take bravery and courage, and require confidence to unlock the opportunities that lie ahead for you in your career.

3. **Inspire belief**

   Research tells us that how confident you appear to others can significantly influence their perception of how competent you are.[19] While we might want to think that doing a good job is enough, the manner in which you do it and how you come across to others is also key to your success. To inspire belief from others you first need to develop the skills so you feel confident internally, and this is then projected externally in how people experience you.

Confidence myths

Before we help you to grapple with your gremlins and build your self-belief, we need to bust a few common myths about confidence.

Myth 1: Extroverts are confident, introverts are shy

Extroversion is often coupled with confidence just as introverts are assumed to be shy. In basic terms the distinction between extroverts and introverts is about how we recharge and where we draw energy from. Introverts tend to recharge by spending time alone, whereas extroverts gain energy from other people and recharge by being social. Whether you are an introvert or an extrovert does not determine how confident you are or how confident you can become.

Myth 2: Confident people are arrogant

There is a difference between confidence and arrogance. To be arrogant is to have an exaggerated view of your own abilities. People who are arrogant lack the self-awareness to accurately understand themselves and the impact they have on others. If you are concerned about developing your level of confidence to the extent where you might become arrogant, it suggests that you are pretty unlikely to get to that point!

Myth 3: Confidence is something you are born with

Some people may have confidence as one of their natural talents, but this doesn't mean they won't still experience moments of doubt or find themselves in situations where they lack confidence. And even where people are naturally confident, they continually improve and hone their skills, as you'll read in Sarah's story about working with Justin King, the CEO of Sainsbury's.

In this chapter, we'll work through the three things that we believe make the biggest difference to your confidence:

1. Understanding and caging your confidence gremlins
2. Recognizing and reflecting on your successes
3. Evaluating and building your support system

Mastering these three things will help build your confidence and an inner sense of self-belief. We end the chapter with some confidence-boosting hints and tips focused on three areas: watch your words, be in your body and practice makes perfect.

Sarah's Story:
Are Kings Born Confident?

When I joined UK retailer Sainsbury's in 2011 the CEO was a man called Justin King. His job was a big one. He was leading an iconic British brand that is 150 years old and which employs over 150,000 people to serve more than 20 million customers every week.

As you'd expect, King's job was a high profile and public one. I watched and listened to him present on a regular basis, whether at one of our leadership updates or in his all-colleague videos. He appeared to be a natural, his manner self-assured, compelling and confident. To me he was one of those people who you assume has been born with innate confidence, and there may be some truth in that, but it's not the whole story. In 2013 I moved to work in the corporate affairs function and had the opportunity to observe how he worked first-hand.

I was surprised. I noticed that, even after years of successfully leading Sainsbury's, he dedicated time to rehearsing and practising, particularly for significant presentations. 'Rehearsal' is the right word to use as he would practise in a way that mirrored a final presentation as closely as possible. A small group of people attended these rehearsals and their job was to provide immediate feedback on both his delivery and content.

I realized that the confidence that King exuded day-in, day-out was a combination of natural talent *plus* hard work and practice.

There is a saying in the retail industry that *retail is detail*, and I think that sums up how he approached his work. He knew that the little things mattered, whether it was choosing the right words for a presentation to motivate others or sending me a handwritten note when I won a leadership award (which I have kept!).

Working with King taught me a few valuable lessons that have stayed with me throughout my career. First, I was relieved to know that it was OK to practise for important moments, as it demonstrates that you understand the impact your confidence can have on other people. Second, that no matter how senior you are, the best leaders never stop learning; they challenge themselves to improve every day. And third, as part of that learning it is useful to ask for and listen to feedback from other people. It shows a respect for the opinions and expertise of others. Everyone can keep learning, even the CEO, and this will improve your performance at work every day.

For King, his approach has certainly paid off. In 2014, when he stepped down from his role, he had led Sainsbury's through thirty-six quarters of consecutive growth – I remember being part of the press office team which received calls from colleagues in-store who wanted to pass on their messages of thanks, not something that happens with your average CEO. He was also awarded a CBE by the queen while at Sainsbury's and since leaving he continues to work in high-profile roles at places including PWC and Marks & Spencer, so his talent and drive continue to pay off.

Step 1: Understanding and caging your confidence gremlins

Confidence gremlins are the things that hold you back from reaching your potential. They get in our way and stop us from doing the things that matter to us. They are the voices in our head telling us we are not good enough, smart enough, experienced enough – and a whole range of niggles that convince us we can't do something. Confidence gremlin is our term for something that is also referred to as 'limiting beliefs'. And we all have them. Other people might not know them or be able to spot them, but they are there lurking in our minds and getting in the way of doing the things that matter to us in our careers.

Your confidence gremlins are unique to you; one person's confidence gremlin can be another person's super strength and vice versa. Or you may have the same confidence gremlin as someone else, but it could hold you back in a different way. For example, two people might have a fear of not being smart enough. For the first person that results in not asking questions and staying quiet in meetings. For the second person the same gremlin shows up as dictating the answers to problems and ignoring other people's perspectives.

Confidence gremlins are the things that hold you back from reaching your potential. Everyone has them, but how you experience them is unique to you.

Though your gremlin is unique in the way you experience it, there are some common gremlins people identify with. See if any of the statements below sound like something you would think about yourself:

I panic whenever I get put on the spot. I freeze and forget what I know.

I don't feel confident about disagreeing with other people as I don't want to be too assertive or unlikeable.

I'm good at what I do until a senior person is in the room; then I get intimidated and lose my confidence.

I hate public speaking. I worry that people are bored or not listening or even worse that they are listening and think I'm not very good at what I do.

I suffer with 'FOBFO' – fear of being found out. I compare myself to other people and think they are better than me.*

I've never been good with numbers, and I avoid asking questions if I don't understand. I even avoid applying for jobs that use phrases like 'commercial acumen'.

* This is often referred to as 'imposter syndrome'.

> There are things I would like to do and am interested in, but I don't pursue them because I'm worried that people will think I'm too young/too old.

> I worry I don't know enough.

> I have a fear of failing. I don't like making any mistakes which means I stay in my comfort zone.

> When I'm under pressure my body gives me away: I blush, get red patches, become sweaty and I get nervous even thinking about it happening.

This might have given you some clues about gremlins you have been dealing with. The following exercises will take you through a step-by-step process to:

- Discover your gremlins
- Identify how they hold you back
- Work out what triggers your gremlins
- Test your gremlin and take positive action
- Reward and recognize your progress

Before you start, know that overcoming your confidence gremlins isn't easy. They represent thoughts you may have had about yourself and how you present yourself for a long time. With ongoing commitment though, they can be tackled and caged and you can stop them holding you back at work.

Discover your gremlins

A useful way to start thinking about your confidence gremlins is to write down the answers to these questions:

1. What are you most afraid of at work?

_____

2. What do you *not* do at work, but wish you did?

_____

3. Fill in the gap: 'I'm not _____ enough to be successful at work.'

4. What negative thoughts do you have about yourself at work?

_____

Sometimes our first idea of what our gremlin might be is not the real gremlin, there is another one lurking deeper below the surface. A good way to discover whether this is the case is to ask yourself a 'why' question at least three times.

For example:

My confidence gremlin is a fear of presenting.

Why do you fear presenting?
   Because I'm worried I'll forget what I'm planning to say.

Why do you worry you'll forget what you're planning to say?
   Because then people will think I'm not very good at my job.

Why do you worry that people will think you're not good at your job?
   Because I want people to think I'm knowledgeable and deserving of my role.

In this example the first gremlin is a fear of presenting, but the root cause of this gremlin is a fear of 'being found out', and that is the most important thing to tackle.

My confidence gremlins

Action: Pick one or two of your potential gremlins and bring them to life by drawing them in the box on page 79.

Drawing your gremlins rather than just writing them down will help to unlock your thinking and enable you to take action. We're not looking for an artistic masterpiece, just a visual representation of how your confidence gremlin shows up or how it makes you feel. Try thinking about what your gremlin would be if it were an animal, for example a giraffe might represent a fear of standing out in a crowd or a hedgehog might represent a fear of being perceived as difficult or 'spiky'. Alternatively, think about an object that could represent your gremlin, such as a stage or spotlight if you fear presenting. If you need some extra inspiration, we've included our gremlins and amateur drawings over the next few pages.

> Asking 'why?' questions will help you to take the most meaningful actions to stop your gremlins getting in your way.

Sarah's Gremlin: Fear of Conflict

My confidence gremlin is a fear of conflict. In my ideal world everyone gets on brilliantly, all of the time, with no friction or arguments. It's not difficult to imagine how this has held me back at work. I would withdraw from any conversation that felt challenging. I would sit in meetings feeling incredibly uncomfortable, partly because of the style of conversation and partly because I would find myself getting hot and sweaty! I would stop listening and afterwards realize I couldn't really remember the content of the meeting. I'd also feel frustrated, as I usually had a point of view to contribute but had missed my opportunity. I avoided spending time with people who, in my mind, I had labelled as my 'conflict culprits', the people whom I blamed for making me feel so uncomfortable.

This fear of conflict was holding me back from things I wanted to do. I was ambitious to lead teams and projects on a significant scale. To do that I needed to demonstrate I had gravitas and could constructively challenge others in the pursuit of the best outcome. As a leader I also wanted to role model the behaviours that I encouraged in my team, and I knew that debate got us to better answers.

There were a few key turning points in my relationship with my confidence gremlin. The first was asking for a simple piece of feedback from a friend I worked with. After a particularly tricky meeting I was moaning to him, but he wasn't really joining in with my venting. I remember asking him, 'On a scale of one to ten, how awkward did you find that meeting?' In my mind the meeting had been an eight or a nine on the conflict scale. He replied, 'Oh it wasn't too bad, probably a three, maybe a four. I was just glad everyone said what they thought in the meeting rather than having corridor conversations, and I think we'll get to a good outcome now.'

His response stopped me in my tracks. That very short conversation helped me to appreciate that my experience of conflict was not the same as everyone else's. Until that point, I had assumed that my feelings were being mirrored by everyone else.

I realized I had been blaming other people for my confidence gremlin rather than taking action and accountability for improving myself.

Challenging my assumptions about conflict was my first step to making some progress. The second step I made was starting to share my gremlin with other people. Initially I felt very vulnerable as I was exposing something I'd spent years trying to keep hidden. My fear was that it could be used against me or be viewed as a sign of weakness. To begin with I only shared my gremlin with a couple of people at work whom I knew well and trusted. These people responded positively, and started to encourage me when I needed it most.

By sharing my gremlin, I had given other people the opportunity to help me in a specific and useful way.

No one judged me negatively, instead people were supportive and sometimes even reciprocated by sharing their gremlins. Sharing my gremlin also meant I was more able to spot my 'gremlin triggers'. I was working on an Amazing If project that wasn't going to plan. After a feedback phone call with one of our clients, Helen commented to me, 'That must have been a hard conversation for you to have but I thought you did brilliantly. I would never have known that you find disagreement difficult.' I was surprised by what Helen had said because I hadn't identified the situation as a conflict scenario, so my confidence gremlin hadn't been triggered. What this helped me realize is that my confidence gremlin is triggered by some specific scenarios and I now know what these are through spending time reflecting on them. The first trigger is unexpected disagreement. When I am in a situation where I anticipate people will agree and the opposite happens, and I'm taken by surprise, my gremlin kicks into action. Secondly, my gremlin is particularly present when I'm dealing with people who have an emotional or direct style of communicating their disagreement.

I've also realized that the language I use to describe my confidence gremlin is really important. I was working with a professional coach and she asked me a profound question that really stuck with me: 'When I say the word "conflict" what's the first thing you think of?' My answer: 'War.' This was a small language point, but it helped me realize that I needed to reframe my confidence gremlin into one that was more appropriate to the situations I found myself in. My confidence gremlin is not conflict. My gremlin is participating in conversations where there are different points of view that I hadn't anticipated, and it is heightened when someone has a style of communicating that is direct or emotional. This is not as catchy as 'conflict', but it is more accurate and is useful in prompting me to take the right actions to ensure that these situations don't hold me back in my career.

To help me work through my gremlin, I have found questions are an incredibly useful way to stay engaged in conversations I find difficult. I keep in mind the mantra 'seek first to understand and then be understood'. I haven't caged my confidence gremlin completely, but I have tamed it to a point where it doesn't hold me back from doing the things I want to achieve in my career.

Identify how your confidence gremlin holds you back

In order to take action, you need to think deeply about what your confidence gremlin is stopping you from doing and how it's holding you back at work. For example, if your gremlin is that you don't know enough then you may be spending hours preparing for meetings, or perhaps you don't speak up in a meeting or ask a question because you worry what other people will think.

Write down three specific situations where your gremlin holds you back at work:

1. _____
   _____

2. _____
   _____

3. _____
   _____

What triggers your gremlin?

Now let's consider specific triggers that prompt your gremlin to appear. If you identified a fear of not knowing enough it could be particular people or meetings where this gremlin typically shows up. Or if you have a fear of presenting, what specific presentations do you try to avoid and make excuses not to do? Work out what your gremlin triggers are and spot patterns for when your gremlin holds you back.

My gremlin triggers

Gremlin	Trigger 1	Trigger 2	Trigger 3
Example: fear of not knowing enough.	Senior people.	People who are good at different things to me.	Being put on the spot.

Testing your gremlin

Our gremlins live in our head and are typically based on assumptions that we haven't tested in the real world. For example, if you have a gremlin about being too young, you might assume people will think you are too inexperienced to apply for a job without ever asking for anyone's opinion. To bring this point to life, here are a few examples of confidence gremlins and their associated assumptions, along with ideas for tests you could take and questions to reflect on.

Confidence gremlin	Assumption	Test	Reflect
I don't know enough.	If I ask a question, I'll look stupid.	Start by practising asking questions in environments where you feel comfortable and with people who know you well. This might be asking your manager more questions as part of your catch-ups.	How did asking a question make you feel, at the time and afterwards? How did other people respond to your question?
I'm not creative.	Other people have better ideas than me.	Share an idea with a positive person in your team and ask for their thoughts on how you could develop it further.	How did it feel to share your idea with someone? Where might your ideas be most useful in your job and organization?

Confidence gremlin	Assumption	Test	Reflect
I don't have enough experience.	I won't be successful or taken seriously if I apply for a job.	Speak to someone who performs a similar role or the person hiring for the role. Test out whether your strengths will add value to the role. Focus on what you can do rather than what you don't have.	How did exploring the opportunity feel? What other similar opportunities could you explore if this role wasn't the right one/you didn't get it?
Add your gremlin here			
Add your gremlin here			

Testing your gremlin kick-starts your ability to make positive progress, because you begin to challenge the beliefs and assumptions that have been holding you back. For example, you might think that your accent makes you less credible, and yet when you get feedback people tell you that your accent actually increases your authenticity and helps people relate to you.

Sometimes though, you might take an action and the result is not what you hoped for and your gremlin feels like it has been reinforced. Let's imagine you had a gremlin about presenting and you pluck up the courage to present at a team meeting, and it doesn't go well. Remember that you are your own worst critic and getting feedback is key to learning. If your own opinion is echoed in the feedback you received (i.e. you thought you could have done better and so did they) then ask people to be as specific as possible about how you could improve. This will help you to take action and develop. As hard as it feels, the best thing you could do in this situation would be to find another chance to present so you can continue caging that gremlin. It is better to get the feedback and improve than allow your gremlin to stop you from trying in the first place.

Taking action is the key to taking control of your confidence gremlin. This is easier said than done, as these gremlins have been around for a while and you have got used to avoiding them.

Overcoming rather than avoiding your confidence gremlins takes positive action, bravery and a deep breath!

Here are a few pointers that can help you to take action:

○ Share your gremlin with someone else (having someone by your side, supporting and encouraging you, will help spur you into action).
○ Be specific about what action you are going to take and when.
○ Make sure your actions are small and frequent.

Use the space below to write down three actions you are going to take to start caging your confidence gremlin, and then circle the action that you are going to take in the next week and who you will share your actions with.

**3 ACTIONS TO CAGE YOUR GREMLIN
(AND CIRCLE PRIORITY ACTION)**

My confidence gremlin
_____

PERSON

The person I'll share
my action with
_____

Recognize your progress

Once you successfully take that first action, make sure you acknowledge your achievement. Any kind of behaviour change is tough, and it takes bravery to start testing long-held beliefs we have about ourselves. So reward yourself for being brave! Each time you take a small action to test a gremlin, come up with a way of patting yourself on the back. The more tangible this can be the better: Sarah likes to indulge herself by buying an artisan coffee and Helen likes to treat herself with new stationery. Keep the reward the same each time you test your gremlin, as it is a great way to remind yourself of the progress you are making.

If you set yourself an action but you weren't quite brave enough (yet!) to take it, don't panic. Reflect on what stopped you. Is the action you set for yourself too much of a leap and you need to start smaller? Is it the right action but the wrong setting? Was it the right action and the right setting and you just need to have another go?

Helen's Gremlin: Fear of Not Being Liked

At some point in my life, I developed an internal narrative that being liked is essential for my career. According to my internal monologue, people have to think that I'm a nice, engaging person in order for me to be successful. Being demanding, difficult or confrontational runs counter to that narrative and therefore I avoid it. The bad news is that this hasn't always played out well in my career. It's meant that I haven't always stood up for what I thought was right, I haven't challenged people when I've had a different perspective and I haven't always given people feedback that could have helped them to improve. The irony is, when I look at other people and see them delivering clear and direct feedback, I think it's great. When I see other people productively challenging others, I admire their approach. When I see other people standing up for what they believe in, I respect their choice. It's just when it comes to me, I'm looking through a different filter. My gremlin of not being liked has been holding me back for a while, but it wasn't until a few years ago that I realized it was holding others back too.

I was working at Microsoft when Kim Scott's book *Radical Candor* come out. I used to listen to the audiobook on my commute into work and one of the feedback styles she said was highly ineffective kept repeating over and over in my mind. The style was being 'ruinously empathetic'. It's where you care personally about the person you are giving feedback to, but you don't challenge directly. As a result, your feedback is ineffective and you prevent the other person from growing, developing and being their best at work. I realized that my need to be liked by the people that worked for me meant that I was delivering ruinously empathetic feedback.

I wasn't confident enough to be clear and direct because of my own gremlin about their perception of me. It was a real breakthrough moment in my thinking.

I started to look at where else my gremlin was affecting other people and I realized it was impacting how confidently I negotiated budgets, pay rises and new working patterns for people. Honestly, I felt ashamed. However, this realization gave me the motivation to tackle my gremlin. From that point forward, I started to take small actions to be more direct and not to turn every statement into a smile. Instead of being ruinously empathetic, I worked hard at developing the skills of 'radical candour'. My team started to feed back to me about how useful they found it and it gave me confidence that I was on the right path.

There have been many difficult conversations since then and I can't say that I've fully caged my gremlin, but being aware that it's there and thinking about its impact on my career and the careers of the people around me keeps me focused on taking small actions and not letting it get in my way. (To read more about radical candour head to Chapter Six: Future Possibilities.)

Step 2: Recognizing and reflecting on your successes

Overcoming your gremlins is only one side of the story when it comes to confidence. To build your confidence you need to know what you are good at and recognize the value you add. Confidence is closely linked to Chapter Two: Super Strengths. If you know and apply your strengths, you will have more successes. Success has a snowball effect. The more successes you have the more confidence you will build.

Most of us are much better at remembering our mistakes than our successes. Confident people who have self-belief are able to reflect positively about the successes they have every day. We can all make a habit out of recognizing the things we achieve in work. To help you do this we have come up with a framework called the three Rs of a success mindset to help develop your confidence: Recognize, Record and Run your own race.

Recognize

Most of us can share one success at work in the last twelve months, but it's often harder to think about a success we had last week, or even yesterday. We can be guilty of defining success in a narrow way and we are often hard on ourselves. A good way to capture all of your success is to think about the different ways and places in which you have success. Try capturing three successes you have had in the last month in each of the following categories (your answers in Chapter Two: Super Strengths might help your thinking here).

Successes at work in the last month:

1. _____

   _____

2. _____

   _____

3. _____

   _____

Example: meeting with a client who shared positive feedback about how much they're enjoying working with me and the team.

Successes at home in the last month:

1. _____
   _____

2. _____
   _____

3. _____
   _____

Example: been to yoga every Tuesday and Saturday.

Helping others to succeed (in and out of work) in the last month:

1. _____
   _____

2. _____
   _____

3. _____
   _____

Example: helped my sister write the introduction to her CV ahead of her beauty course.

This is a great exercise to do as part of a team meeting as well as for self-reflection. Encouraging people to share their successes is a positive way to start any meeting and you often hear examples of achievements that people wouldn't otherwise have the opportunity to share. If you are running this exercise for the first time, let people know before the meeting so they have time to think about what they would like to share (bearing in mind that our successes are rarely top of our minds). And suggest the timeframe for successes, e.g. 'Please come to our monthly meeting prepared to share an example of a success at work, success at home and how you have helped someone else to succeed (at work or home) in the last month.' We have worked with teams who now use this format at the start of their regular catch-ups as they have found it's a positive confidence boost for both individual team members and the group as a whole.

Record

Recording your successes is a simple and effective way to make recognizing them a habit. Try writing down one success at the end of every day for a week – use the notes app on your phone or the notes section at the back of this book. Each day you will find it gets easier to think of a success and by the seventh day you might not even need the prompt of writing it down to know one way in which you've succeeded that day.

Another method for doing this, which can be particularly effective if you are starting a new job or are in a tough environment where you don't feel like you're making much progress, is to do a 'steps forward' and 'steps back' record. Each time you have a success capture this as a step forward, and when something doesn't go to plan, record it as a step back. Every two weeks take half an hour to review your steps forward and backward. Hopefully the first list is longer than the second, and even if it isn't you can think about what you are learning from the second list, which is a success in its own right, so you win either way.

Run your own race

We all know that we should focus on our own successes and not compare ourselves to others (see Emma Gannon's excellent advice in Chapter Eight: 100 Pieces of Career Advice), but this is hard to practise, especially with social media, where our tendency is to share only the positive stuff, editing out the mistakes, failures or boring bits along the way. Understanding what success means to you is naturally something that you will want to reflect on over time, but to get you going start by jotting down the words that spring to mind when we ask: 'What does success mean to you?'

_____

_____

_____

_____

Step 3: Evaluating and building your support system

Building your confidence is not something you can do by yourself. You need a strong support system of people who are there to help you. A Support Solar System is our way of visualizing where your support comes from and where it goes to, and which roles are most significant to you and your confidence. People who are confident have a healthy and balanced support system and evaluating what your system looks like will help you to take meaningful action.

Action: To get started, think about who you receive support from. This can be family, friends and work colleagues, the only caveat is that the support has to be in service of building your self-confidence. Write these names in the first column of the table below. Then, think about who you give support to and write their names in the second column. It's fine to have some of the same people in both columns, but aim for a minimum of five people in each.

Who do you get support from?	Who do you give support to?

Now that you have your list, plot each of these people onto the Support Solar System opposite according to how often you interact with them. This indicates the frequency with which you're either giving or gaining support from that person. Use arrows to indicate the direction of the relationship. Is it someone you give support to (arrow facing away from you), get support from (arrow facing towards you), or is the relationship reciprocal (in which case use a two-way arrow)? We've plotted a couple of examples below to show you how this works.

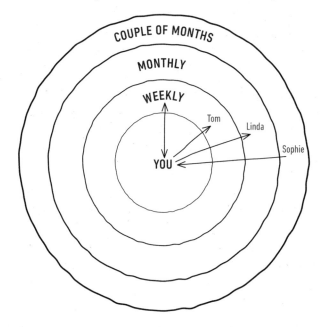

My Support Solar System

Add the people you get support from and give support to below.

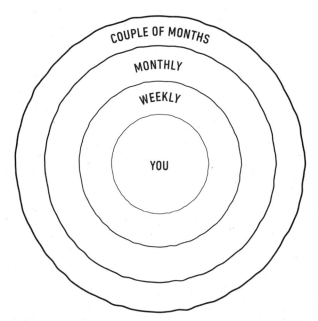

Now that you have mapped out what your current Support Solar System looks like, ask yourself these questions:

- Are you giving more support than you're getting?
- Are you achieving a good balance in the frequency of support you're giving and getting?
- Are you getting support from a diverse range of people, not only family and friends?

This last question is a particularly important one. You are aiming to have a small number of different types of people in your Support Solar System. It is always useful to have someone who unconditionally loves and supports you. Our mums are two of our biggest cheerleaders. It wouldn't matter what we wanted to do, they would believe in us. There is no doubt this makes you feel good, but it is also useful to have people who provide different types of support and challenge you within your support system. Here are some of the types of relationships you want in your Support Solar System:

The person who 'gets' it

Do you have someone giving you support who understands your context? They might work with you now or have worked with you in the past. They can empathize with you and your challenges as they have directly experienced the same or similar environments as you.

The person who asks you the 'hard' questions

Do you have someone who is going to challenge you? This is the person who will ask you brilliant questions, ones that you might not have considered or have been avoiding. These people are useful as they provide you with perspective and stop you falling into the trap of blaming others or becoming a victim.

The person who has 'been there'

We all need a wise owl as part of our support system. These people are usually (though not always) more experienced and have the benefit of time and acquired knowledge. They motivate you to aim high if you are doubting your abilities, they reassure you when things don't go to plan and, like the rest of the people in your Support Solar System, are there for you whenever you need them.

Use the space below to write down the names of people who offer you different types of support in your solar system. This will help you to spot if you have any gaps that you can start to think about filling.

MY PERSON WHO
GETS IT

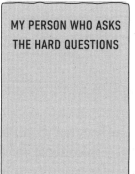

MY PERSON WHO ASKS
THE HARD QUESTIONS

MY PERSON WHO
HAS BEEN THERE

It's also important to reflect on the support you are giving to other people. Knowing who comes to you for support and why can help you to build your confidence and recognize the value you give to others. However, it's a fine balance. If you have too many people that rely on you for support each week, you may be creating dependent relationships that don't help people think through challenges for themselves, and it could also be draining you. If you think you have too many people coming to you for support too frequently, think about other people who might be able to help them or ask them to schedule a monthly or fortnightly catch-up with you. If they share what they would like your support on in advance, it will give you more opportunity to think about how you can help them rather than reacting in the moment.

Step 4: Confidence boosters

We've dedicated the majority of this chapter to helping you build long-lasting confidence. There are also moments where we all need a short-term boost of confidence. In a squiggly career we're going to be doing more jobs and that means more interviews. We'll be working on projects which means working with new people regularly where you want to make a confident first impression. And the increased presence of technology in the workplace means we also need to be confident in our online presence and interactions. We've divided our confidence boosters into three categories: watch your words, be in your body and practice makes perfect. For each of these areas there are three top tips with an example of how taking an action can have a positive impact on your confidence. Underneath each section we've left space for you to write down what confidence-boosting action you want to try out first.

Watch your words

1. **Use confident language in any type of communication.** Avoid in-between words wherever you can, such as: could, should, might, kind of. And use active rather than passive language, like 'I will' rather than 'I think'.

2. **Finish your sentences.** It's amazing how often people don't finish a sentence before moving on to the next point, particularly when you're in a pressured situation and your brain is whirring quickly. Not finishing your sentences is detrimental in two ways: first, your communication will lack gravitas, as confident communicators have clarity and each sentence matters; second, your impact will be reduced, as people won't always intuitively know the point you were going to make. It might have been brilliant, but we'll never know!

3. **Listening matters as much as speaking.** The most confident person in the room isn't necessarily the person who speaks the most. Active listening is incredibly powerful, and it means you can absorb, understand and interpret what is happening in any given situation. Often the people who have the most impact are those that know when to contribute and when to stay quiet!

Watch your words example: Sarah once asked her boss to listen to a presentation she was giving and suggest one idea on how she could give that presentation in a more confident way. Her boss noticed that she used the phrase 'kind of' a lot – and by a lot, she had noticed Sarah saying the phrase at least sixteen times in a ten-minute presentation! Going forward, every time Sarah was tempted to say 'kind of' she practised pausing instead, before continuing her presentation or discussion with a more definitive statement. She still says it occasionally, but hopefully you won't hear it pop up too often on the Squiggly Careers *podcast!*

Watch your words. My action:

Be in your body

1. **Strike a pose.** Many of you might be familiar with Amy Cuddy's work and her TED Talk on body language, which is the second most watched TED Talk of all time. Cuddy's original and subsequent research demonstrates that if you adopt powerful and expansive poses as opposed to powerless, contractive poses before and during an important presentation, meeting or interview, you will feel more confident and powerful as a result.

2. **Get feedback on your body language.** Our body language is often something we aren't consciously aware of. You need to get feedback to understand whether you are achieving the positive impact you are intending. Next time you have a presentation to give, record yourself practising and

play it back – there's nothing quite as revealing as seeing yourself on camera. If you're brave enough, you could even ask someone else to watch or film you and give their feedback.

3. **Take a deep breath or ten.** Taking a deep breath encourages our bodies to release hormones that make us more alert and stimulated. Try breathing in while counting to seven in your head, pause for a second and breathe out for the count of eleven. You should start to feel yourself physically and mentally relaxing. Repeat this breathing exercise ten times. Ten deep breaths will take you three minutes and you should feel an immediate improvement in calmness and confidence.

Be in your body example: Sarah gave feedback to Helen that she often crossed her legs while presenting at workshops they run together. Sarah suggested this was 'closed' body language, so might discourage groups from asking questions. Helen had no idea she stood like that as it was completely unconscious. As soon as she was given the feedback, she realized that it was simply her comfortable standing pose and could easily be changed.

Be in your body. My action:

Practice makes perfect

1. **Rehearse (out loud).** Many of us will spend a lot of time preparing for something we are nervous about. What that usually means is preparing the document or presentation you are going to give and maybe doing additional research, so you are ready for questions. What we underestimate is the fact that how you say something is as important as what you say. Once you get over feeling a little awkward you will find that practising out loud helps you to realize where something doesn't make sense, spot where you're most likely to stumble over words and even where you might need to change some of the content. A useful principle is to practise out loud for three times as long as the presentation you are doing. So, for a ten-minute presentation, practise saying it either out loud to yourself or with a helpful colleague for at

least thirty minutes. You might pause in between each practice to work out what went well and what you'd like to improve.

2. **Practise little and often.** Spot as many different opportunities as possible to practise your confidence. Ask yourself: was the last email I sent a confident one? Have I volunteered for something recently that has helped me to test a confidence gremlin? When was the last time I asked someone for feedback on my confidence, for example: 'Can you tell me when you think I am at my most confident at work?'

3. **Help other people practise their confidence.** By offering to support someone else in developing their confidence, perhaps in an area you have expertise in, you will also inadvertently keep working your confidence muscles. Remember to listen to the advice you are giving others, as we often give our best advice to other people and forget to put it into practice ourselves.

Practice makes perfect example: Before a big presentation, Helen records herself on camera. She then watches it back with the sound on and off. Watching with the sound off helps her to see whether her body language is engaging or distracting. Listening without looking at the screen helps her to hear whether her stories are effective, and the key points are memorable and specific. This level of preparation means that she takes as much control as possible of how she shows up, which increases her confidence on the day.

> **Practice makes perfect. My action:**

Confidence: summary

1 Confidence is a skill. It can be learnt, practised and improved.

2 Confidence gremlins are the things that hold you back at work – and everyone has them.

3 Work out what your gremlin triggers are by looking for patterns of when your gremlin holds you back.

4 To overcome your gremlins, test them by taking small actions.

5 Reward yourself for taking actions to test your gremlins.

6 Confidence and success go hand in hand. The more successes you have the more confidence you will build.

7 The three Rs of building a success mindset: Recognize, Record and Run your own race.

8 Build your Support Solar System to include people who love you, understand you, challenge you and inspire you.

9 Confidence boosters are tactics you can use in adrenaline-fuelled moments to stay calm and self-confident.

10 Our top three confidence boosters are: watch your words, be in your body and practice makes perfect.

'Your network is the
people who want to
help you, and you want
to help them, and that
is really powerful.'

**REID HOFFMAN,
FOUNDER OF LINKEDIN**

Chapter 5
Networks

What is networking?

Networking often falls into the category of things you know you should do to support your career development but don't really want to do or don't know how to do well. For people who don't want to network, it often comes down to how it makes them feel. They may have a sense of dread or anxiety when they think about networking situations and this is largely due to networking being tainted by an out of date view of what it involves. People conjure up images of big events, full of people you don't know, that result in awkward conversations you can't escape from. In reality, this type of networking only accounts for a very small proportion of the ways in which you can build your network, and for some people it might not be relevant at all. For others, they are happy to have conversations with different people about work, but they don't know how to translate it into something that is valuable for their career.

> Networking is simply people helping people.

It's important to remember that networking is simply people helping people. Most of us enjoy the opportunity to help others and this definition can help to reframe what you think about the role and purpose of having a network for your career. To build an effective network you need to be clear about what you can give that is valuable to people and be specific about what help you need and from whom. If you start by being supportive of others you will begin building relationships that can be transformative for your career.

People often make the assumption that networking is just for extroverts, or that it can only be enjoyed by extroverts. That it's only the people who get energy from being with other people (the definition of an extrovert) who can build great networks. This isn't true. Being an introvert or an extrovert is likely to influence how you build your network, but it does not impact the quality or value of building relationships. An introvert may build fewer, deeper, long-term relationships through one-to-one interaction, whereas an extrovert might be more comfortable with and energized by the prospect of a room full of people they don't know yet.

> When it comes to networking, we believe in career karma.
> Focus on what you can give rather than what you hope to gain.

Why networking matters in a squiggly career

Developing the ability to build an active and meaningful network for your career has three significant benefits:

1. Meaningful relationships

Networks used to be made up of people that you had met in person, which meant that while your breadth of contacts might be limited, your network was likely to be small and manageable. Platforms like LinkedIn and Twitter now give us all access to a wide variety of people with whom we might want to build relationships, but might never have met, and this has significantly opened up the networks we can build. However, whether the interactions are virtual or physical, with known or unknown people, the principles of building effective relationships are the same. Having 2,000 connections on LinkedIn does not automatically mean you have a great network. Quantity will never trump quality. Focusing on who you specifically need in your network and investing time in making the relationship valuable for both parties is key to developing a network that helps you in your career.

2. **Diverse perspectives**

In Chapter One: The Squiggly Career, we mentioned the importance of becoming a lifelong learner. People are your richest and most affordable source of wisdom. The only thing you might need to buy them in return for their experience and advice is a coffee or a thank-you card, but their insights can be invaluable. You can leapfrog the learning process by spending time with people who have 'been there and done that', helping you to develop more rapidly and apply your newfound knowledge to your role.

> Building a network based on what you want to learn is a transformative way of thinking about why networking is worth your time and effort.

3. **Building your brand**

As you progress in your career, the majority of your future roles will not come via a jobs board or a company newsletter, they will come from people who know you and understand what you do. Your personal brand is a shortcut that helps people to get a sense of who you are and what you stand for. Being clear about the impression you want to create and acting in a way that is consistent with this is an important part of building an authentic personal brand. As you move around in your squiggly career, your personal brand becomes one of the consistent threads that you take with you.

Building relationships with people inside and outside of your company and profession can also bring unexpected roles and development activities your way; the stronger your relationships are and the more insight people have into your values, strengths and impact, the more likely it is that those opportunities will be a great fit for you. It could be a chance to mentor someone, attend an event or volunteer for an organization you're passionate about. Building and investing in a broad network of people who have insight into you and your personal brand can result in you being a beacon for new and exciting opportunities.

Action: In the space overleaf write down one thing you'd love people to say about you when you're not in the room and three ideas for how you can develop that impression over the next six months.

'I want people to say ———————————————————.'

Actions:
1.
2.
3.

Example: 'I want people to say I'm great at making data meaningful.'
Actions:

1. I could present at an event about the work I've done on reporting.
2. I could write a 'top tips' article on LinkedIn.
3. I could offer to share what I've done in our team with other teams in the business.

Helen's Story: Building a Network of Opportunity

In 2007, I was working as a Marketing Project Manager for Capital One. I had invested time in building the relationships I needed to do my job effectively; I felt like I had done a good job and was ready to progress in a company I loved. I spotted a role advertised for the job of Insight Manager and filled in the application. I was sure that I was the best candidate: I was passionate, keen and believed I had lots of skills that could be transferred to the role. I skipped over the fact that I had no direct experience of working in customer insight, no research expertise and the hiring manager had no idea who I was. You know where this is going … I didn't get the job. Someone in the team took the time to give me some feedback and though I tried to appear receptive, internally I felt defensive and upset. I didn't understand why I hadn't been given the role.

A senior director in the business took me to one side in the week that followed and gave me some blunt but kind feedback. 'You're going about this all wrong,' he said. 'You need to put yourself in a position where the jobs come to you.' I nodded and thought to myself, 'That's fine for you to say, you're a senior director.' But once the disappointment and petulance wore off, I reflected on what he had said. Wouldn't it be amazing if jobs did come to me and what would it take to make that happen? I started to pay more attention to my relationships at work. I became much more curious about people's jobs and careers in other functions and I started to speak to people who did my role in other companies to understand how I could keep learning and improving.

As I moved on from Capital One to E.ON and from E.ON to BP, I invested time in maintaining relationships with the people who had really helped me. An inspiring manager became an ongoing mentor, the colleague I sat next to became a contact I'd bounce ideas off, the internal sponsor became an external advocate. As I progressed as a manager and my teams grew bigger, I continued to support people who worked for me, even as they or I moved on to other roles. I mentored people whom I didn't know but who had reached out to me for support. I spoke at events where people asked for my insights and I started to write and share my point of view in lots of places.

Before I knew it, my network had transformed from a job-specific group of people who helped me to get things done, to a career-specific network that helped me to grow and develop.

Opportunities for new roles and development started to actively come my way. My role at BP came from a headhunter whom someone in my network had recommended me to (we're now friends and continue to help each other), and I used my network to find out what Virgin was really like before I took the position, somewhat ironically, as Head of Insight.

It's more than ten years since those words of wisdom were bestowed on me and my network now couldn't look more different. It's become one of the things I'm known for and it's been fundamental to my development. It's not been a quick process, but I have learnt that it's possible for everyone to build a great network if you consistently and genuinely help others and have the confidence to ask for help in return.

Building a network that works for you

In this chapter, we'll work through the five things that we believe have the biggest impact on building a brilliant network for your career:

1. The three Ds of networking
2. Assessing your network
3. Building your network
4. Creating career karma
5. Understanding your network role

Incorporating these five activities and approaches into your networking efforts will ensure that the time you invest pays back in the short and long term. We will conclude the chapter with some quick tips you can act on to improve your network straight away.

1. The three Ds of networking

There is no formula for the perfect network, and it is not defined by how many people are in it. Your network is unique to you, and you should build it in a way that feels natural, relevant and useful. There are three characteristics that make up a strong network and we recommend keeping these in mind as your start building relationships with people who will actively help you learn and grow.

Discerning

Knowing who can help you learn and grow means you are being conscious about the relationships you are building. You have an awareness of what knowledge you are seeking and have spent some time thinking about who specifically might be able to help you. This means you are intentional, selective and authentic when you build relationships. It's useful to illustrate this point with a practical example.

Finding a mentor is a common action on many people's network to-do list. Over the years we've heard from lots of people who have asked someone for a mentor in this way:

> *I'm looking for a mentor and I wondered if you would consider mentoring me?*

This generic request misses out two pieces of critical information: why they want a mentor and why they feel that particular person would be a good fit. More generally this feels like a request from someone who has perhaps been told to get a mentor or thinks they should because it will look good at work or on their CV. It demonstrates a lack of respect for the other person's time and comes across as lazy. Nine times out of ten this kind of approach receives a 'sorry but no', or no response at all. Time is one of our most finite resources and we need to be mindful of this as we build relationships with people, particularly people who we are hoping can help us in some way.

Let's consider another approach to asking for a mentor, one which is more thoughtful and specific.

> *I'm currently working on developing my gravitas at work. I'm an introvert and find it hard to assert myself in meetings. I read your article on LinkedIn which mentioned being a 'quiet and proud' introvert and it really resonated with how I'd like to feel. I was wondering if you could spare thirty minutes to get together for a coffee or a chat over Skype as I'd love to hear more about your experiences and ask you a couple of questions that I'm struggling to answer for myself.*

This request feels dramatically different to the first one: it's personalized, demonstrates that some self-reflection has already taken place, and is practical (asking for a thirty-minute conversation or a video call rather than a vague notion of mentoring that has no defined start or end). In this scenario the odds are reversed: nine times out of ten people will say yes, as most people like helping other people. And even if someone says no, they will often point you in the direction of someone else who might be able to help.

Deliberate

Your network has to be active. There is an important difference between your network and a collection of people you are connected to. For example, you might have lots of connections on LinkedIn but that doesn't necessarily translate into an active network, just as you might know and say hi to loads of people at work yet fail to connect with them on a deeper level.

An active network is one where you are giving and gaining value, whether that's ideas, time, knowledge or a combination of all three.

Investing in your network takes time, and you will need to be realistic about how much time you have and how best to use that time in order to build a network that works for you.

Dunbar's Number refers to the number of relationships you can meaningfully have at any one point in time. The research, conducted by anthropologist and psychologist Robin Dunbar, suggests we can have one hundred and fifty casual friends, fifty close friends, fifteen people you turn to for support and confide in, and five 'best friends', which often includes family members.[20] These relationships aren't static, they fluctuate and change over time. Though these numbers are focused on personal relationships, it's worth bearing them in mind in relation to your professional network.

We came across a gardening analogy on how to approach networking a few years ago, which states that you should 'seed, feed and weed your network'. The idea of 'weeding' people might feel uncomfortable, but it does acknowledge the need to be deliberate about your network and the time you have to commit to it. You will need to divide your limited time across building new relationships, investing in the right existing relationships and considering whether you need to reduce the amount of time you're spending on some relationships that may now be less relevant for you. Perhaps 'prune' is a better word!

Diverse

We all have a natural tendency towards sameness; it feels safe and comfortable. The danger is that it can be easy to default to a network of people who you enjoy spending time with and who are all quite similar to you. We know that diverse teams perform the best. A McKinsey study of 1,000 companies across twelve countries found that firms in the top quartile for gender diversity are 21 per cent more likely to achieve above average profitability versus the bottom quartile. And this also applies to ethnic diversity, only the figure increases to 33 per cent.[21] The same logic applies to your network: the more diverse it is, the more effective you will find it. Diversity is a broad term and you should apply it broadly when considering your network.

Make sure your network includes people who have different expertise and experience as this will give you fresh perspectives and ideas. It can also help you to learn and develop by exposing you to new concepts and people you would otherwise have been unaware of. Make sure you aren't filtering your network too narrowly and that it isn't based solely upon people who work in your industry or profession. And remember: diversity of experience also includes people less experienced than you. Someone starting out in their career will offer you a different perspective, one unencumbered by knowing how things currently work or assumptions about what the right answer to a particular opportunity or challenge should be.

We all have our own style at work, which reflects our strengths and values. For example, you might be someone with a particularly collaborative and friendly style. Or you could be someone who is known for brilliant problem-solving and attention to detail. Some of us rely more on intuition at work whereas others prefer to base our decisions on facts. When considering your network make sure you include people who work and think in a different way to you. It can feel challenging to spend time with these people, but they will ask you questions that prompt you to think in a different way and encourage you to spot possibilities that broaden your horizons.

2. Assessing your network

Before you can begin building your network, you need to start by considering your network today. Where do you have strong relationships and what gaps can you spot? These gaps represent opportunities for improvement. One way to evaluate your network is to assess the strength of the three networks that are most powerful for your career development:

1. Current role network – the people who help you succeed in your job
2. Future role network – the people who help you explore career possibilities
3. Personal development network – the people that help you to be your best

Once you have assessed the strength of your network today, you can identify what actions you want to take over the next twelve months to build the relationships that matter most to you right now.

Step 1
Start by completing the chart below, indicating a score of zero to five for how strong each of your networks are today: zero means you don't think you have any network today and five means it's very well developed. Before you score, remember the point we made about limited time; unless you're treating networking as a full-time job, it's unrealistic to have five out of five across all three areas. Join each of your three marks together to create a triangle illustrating the current shape of your network.

Step 2
Now, think about where you would like those scores to be in twelve months' time and plot that onto the diagram too, this time using a dotted line. You might be happy with where you are with a particular network today, and in that case the score won't change. Again, join up each of the three marks to create a second triangle.

Your network today and in twelve months' time
Now that you have completed the exercise you can identify in which area you have the biggest network gap between where you are today and where you want to be. Or you might have a couple of gaps that are the same. We would suggest that you don't try to improve all three networks simultaneously. Instead, prioritize which area you would like to focus on, depending on what your career priorities are over the next twelve months. You might choose to focus all your energy and time on your priority gap,

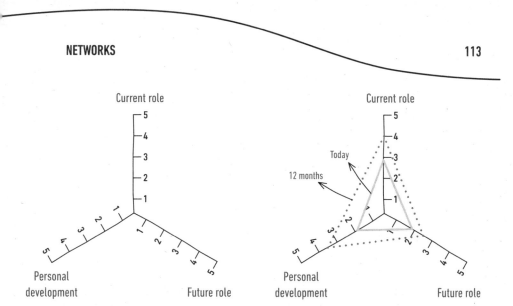

or you might like to focus on, developing two areas, with more emphasis on one. Work out what feels most useful and realistic for you at the moment. Identify your priority network gap (and secondary, if relevant) and circle it in the action box below.

> **My priority network gap is:**
> current role | future role | personal development
>
> **My secondary network gap is:**
> current role | future role | personal development

Filling the gap

Now that you have an idea where your network gaps are, let's explore the actions you can take to improve in these areas. We would suggest reading the ideas for each of the three networks, not just for your priority network gap, as it might spark a new idea that will help your network to get even stronger.

3. Building your network

Current role network actions

If you are new in your current role this can often be the reason for a lower score in this area, as you haven't had the time to build the right relationships yet. Typically, this tends to be people's highest score, as your current role network naturally grows through going to work each day. However, we are often too narrow in our approach to building a current role network. Consider the actions we've recommended to make sure you are actively investing in the right relationships to be at your best in your role.

Action 1: Create the right relationships for you and the people around you

We often focus our energy on the direct relationships we need to do our jobs well. This is important and usually the priority, but we need to recognize that there is a wider ecosystem of relationships for us to consider. As a team it is useful to do a stakeholder mapping exercise to visualize and prioritize the relationships you need across a particular group or function. Using an impact versus influence matrix (you can Google what one of these looks like) can help you to structure this conversation. An alternative approach is to ask your peers and your manager, 'What relationships do I need to build to help you do your job effectively?' The same question applies if you are leading a team: what relationships do you need to build so both you and your team can be brilliant?

Action 2: Develop the right external relationships for your role

A strong current role network includes both internal and external relationships. To build a network that will support you to be the best at your job, you will need to invest in relevant relationships outside of your organization, whether that be industry experts, thought leaders, partners or even competitors. It is incredibly important to have what we refer to as 'meerkat moments' in our jobs.

Meerkat moments are times when we poke our heads up outside our organization in search of inspiration, ideas and opportunities.

If this is an area where you want to take action you could invite someone with the same job as you but in a different industry to come and speak at your next team meeting (and then reciprocate). Or you could identify industry meet-ups or professional bodies that you could get involved in.

Action 3: Make your super strengths known (see Chapter Two)

Your current role network will be much more powerful for your career if people know what you're great at. This can turn a relationship with someone from a nice catch-up over coffee to a more focused discussion which may result in opportunities to use your strengths in new and impactful ways at work. Talk proactively with people about how you're using your strengths to add value at work and share ideas for how you could help them in their roles too. Ask them if they have any thoughts on how you could use your strengths more. This will have the double benefit of establishing your strengths in their mind and leading to new ways to increase the frequency with which you use them at work.

Future role network actions

You might have given this network a low score because you aren't sure what you want to do next or you are quite content with where you currently are. However, if you only start developing your network when you want a new job, you've left it too late. You should be investing in your future role network long before you are ready to make your next move.

Action 1: Share your interests

People can only help you if they know how to help. Be specific about what you are interested in, and you will be amazed at the opportunities to experiment and learn that will come your way. Write down five things you are passionate about in the context of your work: for example, leadership approaches, creative thinking, project management or neurodiversity. Then, start telling people that you are interested in those areas and asking if they know anyone you could speak to in order to learn more about them. Not only will this plant your passions in their mind, it will also help to connect you to new people who may be able to spot development or career opportunities for you.

1. ————————————————————————
2. ————————————————————————
3. ————————————————————————
4. ————————————————————————
5. ————————————————————————

Action 2: Start a side project

Side projects have become more prominent over the past few years and we talk more about the pros and cons of them in Chapter Seven: Squiggly

Career Conundrums. Aside from potentially bringing in an additional source of revenue, one of the undoubted benefits of a side project is the chance to build your network with new people. In the context of your future career, a side project gives you the opportunity to experiment, build your profile and reputation, and get to know people in a new area. Side projects give you the chance to connect with people on a topic you are passionate about, and that's often the point at which networking stops becoming a thing you feel you should do and becomes about building meaningful relationships.

Action 3: Go to where people already are

Whether your future career possibility is becoming a vet or an animator, chances are there will be physical and virtual networks that already exist that you can get involved in. Participating in existing networks gives you the opportunity to explore career options with people who are already living and breathing it. It is also a less pressurized environment than an interview, so you'll probably find people are more honest about the pros and cons of a company or industry than they might be in more formal situations.

The best way to explore future career possibilities is with a curious and open mindset. Find out where people who are interested in the same career opportunities as you hang out. Are there online forums you could contribute to, speaker events you could attend or experts you could follow on LinkedIn? Once you start being proactive and taking action you will find that one thing leads to another and in a relatively short space of time you can make a lot of progress in building a network of people who will help you with future roles.

Personal development network actions

A strong personal development network means building relationships with people who help you to be at your best. These people support your development in a number of ways: challenging you, giving you honest feedback and providing a confidence boost at the moments you need it the most. Often, people worry that personal development relationships feel one-sided, with one person doing all the giving and the other person all the gaining. This is rarely, if ever, the case. These relationships usually offer the opportunity for both parties to learn and develop together.

Action 1: Build a portfolio of 'meaningful' and 'of the moment' mentors

We recommend building a portfolio of two different types of mentors: 'meaningful' and 'of the moment'. A meaningful mentor is someone you build a relationship with over a significant period of time, years rather than months. These people will support you across a number of different roles and organizations during your career. You will only have a few meaningful mentors, as these are deep and trusting relationships that require high levels of investment from both the mentee and mentor. Meaningful mentors may well start off as an 'of the moment' mentor and grow organically over time, based on personal chemistry and the people you 'click' with.

In contrast, your 'of the moment' mentors are situational and specific. These are mentors that you identify because they can help you learn or improve in an area they have experience of. This could be a skill, behaviour, industry knowledge or a combination of all three. These people are highly relevant to you at a particular moment in time. Your relationship with 'of the moment' mentors is likely to be shorter, but it might still last for several years. As an example, in 2018 when Sarah moved from working in big brands to leading a small and fast-growing creative agency, she sought out an 'of the moment' mentor who had made the same transition. This relationship was particularly useful in the first twelve months of Sarah's role and has now become more ad hoc, as and when Sarah has a specific area she'd like to discuss.

Action 2: Earn a sponsor

A sponsor is a person who advocates for you. Sponsors are often, though not always, your boss, and the relationship works differently to the one you have with a mentor. Sylvia Ann Hewlett, an author, CEO and educator on sponsors, defines the difference as 'mentors advise and sponsors act'. Her research has demonstrated that people who have a sponsor are more likely to ask for a stretch role and are more confident in negotiating a pay rise.[22] The biggest challenge in getting a sponsor is that you can't ask for one, their advocacy is earned. There are two actions you can take to earn a sponsor: spot them and work out what you want to be sponsored for. In every organization there are some people who are visible champions of others, both of their own team members and other individuals across the organization. Look out for who these people are and explore opportunities to work together, or even to be part of their team in the future.

Sponsors will talk specifically about what you do well and the value you add, so be clear in your mind about what you want your sponsor to say about you when you are not in the room. For example, someone saying 'Helen is great' is OK, but not an example of proactive sponsorship. Instead, you are aiming for something more along the lines of 'Helen excels at leading teams that need to drive change, she is highly committed to developing people and she approaches everything she does with energy and purpose'. You need to make sure your sponsor is seeing your strengths in action to legitimately champion you in this way.

Action 3: Discover your learning tribe

Seek out people who want to learn the same things as you to add to your personal development network. You can do this by searching for existing groups in an area you are interested in, for example finding a meet-up for people learning to speak a new language or learning how to draw. Or it can be as simple as finding a learning buddy in your organization who is interested in the same things you are. Share your learning priorities with other people and ask them about theirs. This will help you to connect to people who share your passion. Learning with others is powerful as it makes the learning active, two-way and more likely to stick.

4. Creating career karma

As clichéd as it sounds, in our experience good things happen to people who do good for others. And when it comes to networking this means people who give without the expectation of immediate return. Adam Grant's research into high achievers demonstrates that the one thing they have in common is that they take determined action to achieve their own ambitious goals *and* routinely contribute to the success of others.[23] In other words, they are givers, people who are generous with their time and expertise and go out of their way to help others succeed. When you focus on what you can give others you are building up credit in your 'network bank'. And when you work on what you can give in a way that uses your strengths and matches your passions, networking becomes something you can enjoy and even look forward to. After all, it's just people helping people.

GIVE and get

You might be reading this thinking, 'I like the idea of people helping people, but I don't have anything to give.' We know from our experience in workshops that everyone has something to give. Even by reading this book you have, we hope, learnt some useful career development tools and techniques that you could pass on to someone else, but your list will be much longer than that. The real trick here is to translate your strengths into something that could be interesting and useful for other people.

For example, perhaps you have been running a side project or volunteering for the last few years. You could use the knowledge you have gained to run a session or write a blog on the five steps you took to start your side project; you could write an article about what volunteering means to you and why it matters. Or perhaps you are passionate about coding and could use your skill and enthusiasm to help other people develop a basic competence as well as building your profile around your coding expertise.

Your strengths and passions are a valuable starting point to thinking about what you have to give, and we'll use this insight in the next exercises in this chapter.

Your give generator

Even if you've not yet read Chapter Two: Super Strengths, you probably have some idea of the things you are good at and the areas you enjoy and

My strengths/passions	How could this be useful for other people?
Copywriting	1. Start writing a monthly blog post on how anyone can improve their copywriting. 2. Offer to write a newsletter for an industry group that I'm part of.
Developing others	1. Buddy up with new people who join my organization and have weekly catch-up coffees for three months. 2. Complete a different skillshare course every month and share the highlights with my team at work.
Being organized	1. Ask the organizers of events that I've attended and enjoyed if they need any volunteers to help organize events in the future. 2. Volunteer to support my manager in organizing team days and social events.

are interested in. Use the table below to write down three of your strengths or passion areas. For each strength, then write down two ideas of how you could turn it into something that will be useful for other people. We've included a few examples on the previous page to help you get started.

My strengths/passions	How could this be useful for other people?
	1. 2.
	1. 2.
	1. 2.

All the actions you have identified have two things in common: they require your time and your energy. This is why it is important for you to prioritize which actions you want to take. You could prioritize based on the strength you feel most confident in, or the idea that feels most interesting to you, or what you think might be most helpful to others. Circle the idea you want to prioritize and take action on in the next month.

Give and GET

Understanding what help you're looking for from others, i.e. what you want to 'get' from your network, means you can connect with the right people and successfully ask for their support. To get started, think about how you would answer the following question:

What are the three things I'd like to learn in the next twelve months that will help me develop and grow in my career?

It might be knowledge about your profession, how to develop certain skills, or the way another organization works. The more specific you can be about this the better. So, instead of 'I want to learn how to be a better presenter' try 'I want to learn how to use storytelling to improve how I engage people when I present'. This statement has a more specific learning objective and also references why you want to learn it. Write down three learning objectives in the left-hand column of the table below.

Learning objective	Who can help?
1.	
2.	
3,	

Once you have your three ideas, you can then think about who could help you and fill out the right-hand column. There are three ways to figure out who can help you.

1. **Speak to the people you already know.** Don't underestimate how useful your current network can be once you have been specific about what you are hoping to learn. And don't assume what people can and can't help you with. You never know who people are connected to, or the previous experience people might have that could be useful.

2. **Do your research and find the experts.** Before you speak to anyone to ask for help, make sure you've done your research. With so much information readily available it's easy to do some initial exploring for yourself. People are more willing to offer support if they feel that the person approaching them has done some thinking and research for themselves first. The point of speaking to an expert is that they can add value in a way that you couldn't access elsewhere.

3. **Ask a connector to join the dots.** Look out for the people that have strong networks. Let them know what help you are looking for and ask them either for inspiration or to make a connection on your behalf. Sharing your priority learning objective with a person who is a natural connector is useful as they will then be on the lookout for other people who can help you.

Action: For each of your learning objectives decide on the first person in your network that you are going to approach for help and write their name in the right-hand column of the table above.

Once you know who to ask for help, it's important to know how to ask, so we've outlined some tips on asking and what to do if someone says no.

How to ask for help: be thoughtful, clear and make it easy

You are far more likely to be successful in your request if you can be specific about what help you need and why you are contacting them. Also consider letting the person know what you have already done to learn independently; this will show you are committed and genuine about wanting to learn.

Think about the timing of your request. If you know someone is working on a big project or they work in finance and you're contacting them at year end, responding to you might not be top of their to-do list. Finally, don't make them guess about how best to help you. If you want a meeting, ask for it. If you want a call, say so. Be thoughtful. Be clear. Make it easy for them to say yes. Follow these principles and the majority of people will find some way to help.

How to respond to 'no'

Despite all of your hard work, there will still be situations when people say no. This is not a reflection on you and there are likely to be good reasons behind a 'no'. If someone says no, don't feel angry or defensive. Instead, let them know you understand and, if it feels appropriate, you can always ask for a recommendation for someone else who might be able to help. 'I understand, thank you for letting me know. Is there anyone else you could recommend that I could speak to?'

How to respond to a 'no reply'

You may also be faced with a different kind of 'no': the frustration of the 'no reply'. There are many reasons for a 'no reply'. It might be that the person isn't interested in helping, they haven't seen your request, they are overwhelmed with requests and aren't able to reply to them all or they saw it and forgot to reply. After a message, wait a couple of weeks before doing a follow-up. Sometimes people do want to help but genuinely forgot or missed your message in the midst of a particularly busy week.

If you can spot an opportunity to prompt your final follow-up then that's even better. For example, if someone tweets or posts an article or update online, you could reference that in your follow-up note:

> I really enjoyed your recent article on flexible working, especially the point on focusing on the 'how' rather than the 'why'. I got in touch a couple of weeks ago as I would be really interested to chat to you more about how I could implement flexible working in my organization. If you don't have time right now, no problem, and if there is anyone else you could recommend I speak to that would be great.

The tone of this note demonstrates that you understand someone is busy and appreciate they might not be able to connect with you at that moment. And if you don't get a reply, don't take it personally or let it knock your confidence. Move on to the next person or network who you think might be useful.

5. Understanding your network role

As you become more confident in building relationships, it is important to choose the role you want to play in any network you are part of. There are four roles to consider.

Role 1: The Consumer

If you're a consumer, it means that you are joining a pre-existing network and taking value from what's already there. This can be valuable, and you will probably learn something from the experience, but the principle here is more about 'people helping you' rather than 'people helping people'. Being a consumer at networking opportunities can be a good way to build up your confidence, as it's the easiest and least pressurized way of engaging with a network. Just make sure you are not spending 100 per cent of your networking efforts here though, as you are unlikely to be building relationships that will help you in your career development if you are solely in 'consume' mode.

Role 2: The Contributor

A contributor is someone who is putting something into a network. It could be their time, ideas or offering up their skills and expertise where they see a useful opportunity. When you are a contributor you are taking an active part in a network and deepening your relationships with people. Contributing to a network can be as simple as inviting someone you know to be part of a group you belong to because you think they will have something to give and gain. Or if you want to contribute further you can always ask someone who runs a network how you can help. Running a network of any shape takes a lot of hard work and dedication, so any offer of support is usually gratefully received.

Role 3: The Connector

Connectors play a powerful role in networks. Their networks have become so strong that they are now able to connect people together. These people are hubs and you'll often hear other people talking about them. Being a connector is rewarding, and great connectors tend to enjoy the process. If this is something you'd like to spend more time on, start thinking about who you could proactively connect in your current network. Could your new boss learn from your old boss? Could someone you mentor get value from someone else in your team? Connecting people is as simple as an email or LinkedIn message with a short introduction and your perspective on how you think both people could benefit from knowing each other.

Role 4: The Creator

The most challenging way of building your network is to create your own. The effort this takes shouldn't be underestimated and sometimes the situation can snowball when you find something that lots of people are interested in. However, the benefits are that you have high visibility in the network, you own the relationships and you can shape the focus of the network so it aligns with your learning objectives.

We have both created networks and have learnt a few things about how to go about it and what not to do. The first is just to start! Don't think about it too much, keep it small, and if it's interesting people will come and begin bringing and receiving value as consumers or contributors. The second is to bring other people in to help you with the network so the effort of managing it doesn't overwhelm you. The third is to talk about the network you have created when you're building relationships with people. People are often attracted to you because of the initiatives you choose to engage in outside of your day job.

Action: Now you know the four roles, write down what percentage of time you spend in each role in the boxes below. Think about whether that is the right balance for you and if there are any percentages you would like to increase or decrease.

Consumer __%	Contributor __%
Connector __%	Creator __%

Quick-fix tips and tricks

Building a strong network is an essential skill for your squiggly career. It takes time and effort and is a continual work in progress. In addition to the actions we have already shared, here are some more tactical tips and tricks that will help you improve your networking (aka people helping people).

For events

1. **Look for the odd one out.** If you're at an event on your own, scan the room for someone on their own or in a three. If they are on their own, they are probably feeling as awkward as you and if they are in a three, there is likely to be one person whose attention you can capture.

2. **Buddy-up.** If you are nervous about attending an event by yourself, use it as an opportunity to extend an invitation to a friend who might also enjoy the event.

3. **Research.** See if you can get hold of an attendee list before arriving. This can reassure you that you already know some people attending, or there might be someone you'd specifically like to meet that you can look out for, or even send a message to prior to the event.

For one-to-one relationships

1. **Curate knowledge.** Find articles or books that you think someone would find valuable and go beyond just sending them a link. Instead, take the time to identify some specific insights, quotes or take-aways you think are interesting and relevant to them.

2. **What's the problem?** Think about a problem that person is trying to solve currently and how you could help them. Then get in touch with them to share your ideas.

3. **Stay alert.** If there is a specific person you want to build a relationship with and they are senior or have a significant profile, consider setting up a Google alert for their name or business. This means you will always be up to date with any significant business events that they are involved in and can have a relevant conversation with them when the opportunity arises.

For virtual networks

1. **Engage.** Start commenting on, tagging and sharing content from a targeted list of social media profiles. Over time, this can create a dialogue with the individual or community that you can build a relationship from.

2. **Invite opinion.** When you share an article you have read or a post you have written, ask for people's thoughts to generate two-way conversation.

3. **Get visual.** Use a headshot or video wherever possible, in your profile picture and your posts, so people can see you behind the screen. This makes you more human and relatable and crosses the chasm between physical and virtual interaction.

Networks: summary

1 Networking is people helping people.

2 In a squiggly career, your network helps you to develop meaningful relationships, gain access to diverse perspectives and build your brand.

3 Everyone can build a successful network whether you are an introvert or extrovert. The best relationships are built authentically and in a way that feels right for you.

4 To build a brilliant network you need the three Ds: to be discerning, deliberate and diverse in your approach.

5 Assess the strengths and gaps in your network by identifying the relationships you have which support your current role, career possibilities and personal development.

6 The best networks are built on what you can give without expectation of immediate gain.

7 To identify what you can give to a network, start with your strengths and passions and how these can be useful for other people.

8 Not everyone will say yes to networking requests; don't be disheartened or take it personally.

9 Know what role you are playing in a network: consumer, contributor, connector or creator.

10 Developing a successful network takes time, energy and is a continual work in progress.

'Don't feel guilty if you don't know what you want to do with your life ... the most interesting people I know didn't know at twenty-two what they wanted to do with their lives, some of the most interesting forty-year-olds I know still don't.'

BAZ LUHRMANN

Chapter 6
Future Possibilities

What are future possibilities?

It might be easier to start with what they are not. Future possibilities are not rigid plans or fixed destinations; they are not answering the question, 'What job do you want to be doing in five years time?' Career plans may have been appropriate for a predictable world of work where you could envisage the future with a high degree of certainty, but they are not fit for squiggly careers. We can no longer rely on the tried, tested and trusted formula for work: hard work + loyalty = promotion (and then repeat until retirement).

As Lynda Gratton, professor at London Business School and co-author of the excellent book *The 100-Year Life* points out, the concept of a three-stage life – education, work and then retirement – is fast disappearing. Gratton suggests that we are moving towards a world where multiple transitions will become the norm, requiring us to be flexible, acquire new knowledge and explore different ways of thinking. A recent *Financial Times* article outlined that we should plan for five careers in a lifetime, and that as work is becoming more impermanent, reinvention is both rational and essential.[24]

> Squiggly careers are fluid, not fixed.

This fluidity is having an impact on our relationships with our employers too. When we both started our careers the notion of going 'back' to a previous employer was frowned upon, as it was considered a 'backward' step in your career. Now, however, we are seeing an increase in 'boomerang' employees who return to a previous employer. One example of this is Biz Stone, the founder of

Twitter who, having sold his business in 2011, returned in 2017 to once again lead the company with a particular focus on culture.

Our careers are becoming multi-directional as we move back and forth, in and out of organizations and professions. Progressive organizations recognize that people leave for a variety of reasons, from career advancement and broadening experiences to working in another geography or starting up a business. Employee retention is no longer the only indicator of a happy workforce.

Ditch the destination

We need to shift our focus from plans and destinations to one where we are discovering opportunities and enjoying the journey. Any kind of plan suggests there will be a point where an outcome is achieved. For many, success is defined by achieving that outcome. However, this thinking is broken logic for a happy career. Shawn Achor, the positive psychologist and author of *The Happiness Advantage*, challenges the assumption that success leads to happiness and argues that it happens the other way around: it's the people who are the happiest, that focus on enjoying the journey and not obsessing over the destination, that are the most successful in the long run.

If career plans are not the answer, then what is? Should we ignore our future careers and instead focus our energy on enjoying the present? Perhaps, but it leaves a lot to chance and it's a big risk to take with something as important as our careers. Instead, we need to approach our future work by embracing the squigglyness we experience today. We need to forget about plans and focus on possibilities.

Why do future possibilities matter in a squiggly career?

Understanding and exploring your possibilities will help you in your future career in three ways:

1. **Taking ownership**

   The changing relationship we have with our employer and the unpredictable nature of work means that it is more important than ever to take control of your career. You cannot rely on your manager or your employer to provide a clear career path for you; those career paths are unlikely to exist for much longer. Instead, you need to combine everything you have learnt about yourself in this book and use your insights to explore and connect this to different roles you may explore in the future.

2. **Discover opportunity**

   Exploring future possibilities allows us to get curious about different roles and organizations. A career that might have seemed linear and limited can be opened up when you think about all the different places your strengths could create impact. When you connect this with your values you can uncover career possibilities that you may never have considered before. Thinking creatively about your career can unlock unlimited possibilities for your future.

3. **Finding a good fit**

   Career change in any direction inevitably comes with some risk. Whether it's a horizontal internal move or a pivot into a new industry, digging deeper into whether the opportunity is a good fit for your strengths, values or career must-haves will make it more likely to be a successful transition. Reflecting on these areas can also help you to have a more balanced perspective and ensure you are moving towards a new role, rather than running away from your current one.

We've divided this chapter into two parts. In part one we focus on two different exercises, future possibilities to help you explore career options, and finding your career 'why', which will help guide your career choices. In part two we focus on three 'up and coming' career skills – curiosity, feedback and grit – that we predict are only going to become more important as the world of work, and your career, continue to be squiggly.

Part One –
Possibilities

Future possibilities are the areas of work that you are interested in exploring as potential job roles. Some of these possibilities might feel very familiar to you, whereas others could be relatively unknown. Either way, a possibility is something you are curious to know more about.

To discover your possibilities, you need to adopt an exploring mindset, be open and think creatively about a number of different potential futures. While we want some of the possibilities to feel relatable from where you are today, we will also encourage you to think imaginatively about your options.

You can explore as many career possibilities as you find useful, but to get you started here are four different types of possibilities to consider:

1. **Your obvious possibility.** This is usually the easiest possibility to imagine. It's whatever the obvious next step is from what you're doing today. This does not necessarily mean a promotion; the obvious next step could be a sideways move to broaden your experience. Your obvious possibility is whatever feels intuitively like the next natural step in your career.

2. **Your ambitious possibility.** This is the role you might have been thinking about in the back of your mind, however it often comes with a 'but'. So that thought process might sound something like, 'I guess I could do my manager's job, but they have much more experience than me' or 'I could switch from working in a big company to a start-up, but I don't know anyone else who has made that move successfully'. Imagine 'but' didn't exist; what possibilities would you explore?

3. **Your dream possibility.** If you had no constraints, what work would you be doing? This is where you can have some fun, as the only caveat is that you have to work. It could be something similar to what you're doing today, or it might be radically different, such as a banker becoming a chef, an admin assistant becoming a police officer, a factory worker becoming a gardener (these are all real examples from people we know!).

4. **Your pivot possibility.** This is focused on finding roles where you could apply your existing skills and strengths in a new way. This means thinking laterally about other places where your strengths could make a positive impact. This could be in a different type of organization, for example moving from the private to the public sector, moving from full-time office work to freelancing, or from a corporate career to a consulting role, or it could be breaking into an entirely new industry.

Write down one idea for each possibility below.

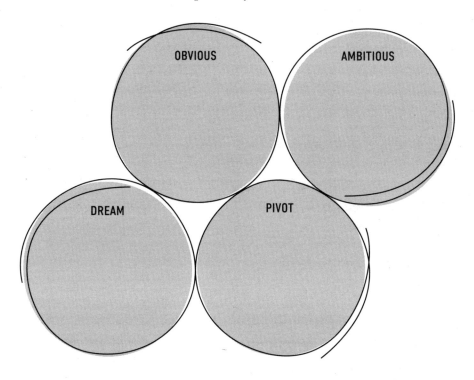

Now that you have identified some future possibilities, the next step is to work out what actions to take to explore them.

Action: Choose one of the possibilities you would like to start exploring straight away and jot down your thoughts on the two questions below:

- What do I need to know?
- Who can help me?

The first question involves making a list of all the gaps in your current knowledge. What will you need to find out as part of your exploring process? As this is a new possibility for you it is likely that there will also be some 'unknown unknowns', where you're thinking, 'I don't know what I don't know'. This is where the second question helps. Think about all the people in your network who can help you learn more about a possibility; then think further afield than your existing network – the people who can help you don't always have to be people you know. Discover who the thought leaders in your possibility are and start reading, watching and listening to their work.

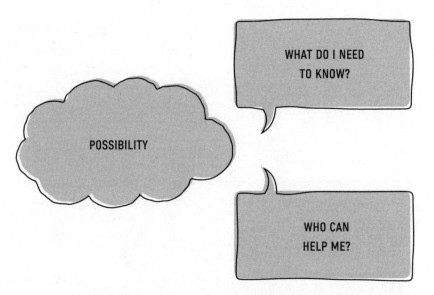

Over time you will discount some possibilities, add other ones and might even find that something that was once your dream possibility becomes an ambitious one, or a pivot possibility might become your next obvious role. Exploring your possibilities takes time and energy so it is useful to think about which ones you want to prioritize at the moment. You might be proactively exploring your ambitious possibility and keeping an eye out for opportunities to learn more about your pivot possibility. By consciously identifying possibilities you will find yourself naturally spotting chances to start discovering more; whether that is people you want to meet, events to attend, books to read or courses to sign up to.

Your possibilities don't stand still and neither do you.

Five possibility prompts

We have come up with five possibility prompts that will help as you start exploring future roles. For each prompt there are two questions: one to reflect on for yourself and one that you can ask other people. You will notice that each of these prompts and questions are connected to the four other squiggly career skills (strengths, values, confidence, networks) that we have discussed in this book.

1. Strengths possibility prompt

Self-reflection question: How will the career possibility you are exploring give you the opportunity to use your strengths regularly and in particular your super strengths?

Question to ask: What are the skills and behaviours that are most valuable and useful in this role?

2. Values possibility prompt

Self-reflection question: How will this career possibility mean you can be yourself at work and live your values?

Question to ask: Some of the things that are important to me about what/where/who I work with are _____. How well do you think these things fit with working in this industry or company?

3. Confidence possibility prompt

Self-reflection question: How will this possibility build your confidence?

Question to ask: What are some of the challenges of the job that require the most resilience from you and the team?

4. Networks possibility prompt

Self-reflection question: How will this possibility mean you can use your network 'gives' and get access to your network 'gains'.

Question to ask: Are there any gaps in knowledge or skills that you're trying to fill at the moment?

5. Future possibility prompt

Self-reflection question: How will this possibility lead to other interesting career possibilities for you to explore?

Question to ask: How can you see this team evolving in the future?

Sarah's Story:
From Masterplan to Maternity Leave

I love to plan. I've completed the Myers–Briggs personality type indicator* a number of times over the years and the one thing that never changes is that I have a strong 'J' preference. The J stands for judging, which doesn't mean judgemental (thankfully) but it does mean that I like to be organized, make decisions and take control. A few examples to bring this to life: I handed in my final MBA assignment a month early, in January I block out my holidays for the year ahead in my calendar and I always aim to arrive at meetings ten minutes before they are due to start.

In 2010, while working at Barclays, I decided that I needed to create a career plan. My career plan was a self-proclaimed masterpiece, detailing exactly what was going to happen in my career over the next five years. I was proud of my plan and sat down with my manager to talk her through it. After listening carefully she asked, 'Why do you want to do each of these things on your plan?' Ummmmmmmm. So, the honest answer was I had listed all the things I thought I needed to do in order to achieve the ultimate job title I was aiming for. The plan had no relevance to my strengths, the things I enjoyed or was interested in. Essentially it was a list of

---

* You can do a version of the Myer–Briggs personality indicator test for free at 16personalities.com.

things I thought I should do, rather than things I wanted to do. Rather than discourage me, my boss gave me the opportunity to attend an event called Gather in London, a leadership conference with an impressive line-up of speakers. One particular speaker stood out for me, a woman called Cilla Snowball. Cilla talked about not having a career plan but instead being clear about the value you add in any role in an organization.

She urged people to think carefully about each career choice but equally to bear in mind that as long as you were going to be happy and learning you couldn't go too far wrong.

Her down to earth, approachable and honest style had a lasting impact on me. From that point onwards I changed tack, moving from career plans to possibilities.

Fast-forward nine years and I'm eight months pregnant. At which point it's announced that the marketing division I am working in is going through a significant restructure that impacts pretty much all of my team and my own role is disappearing. I get offered the opportunity to apply for a role which is similar to something I've done before, and decide it doesn't feel like the right choice for me. Instead, as I went on maternity leave, I left the company permanently, with no role to go back to and no idea what I would do next. Even though it was a tough situation I felt OK and even excited about what would come next. Since changing my mindset from rigid career plans to exploring possibilities, I had learnt to see a number of different options available to me. I realized I could spend more time building Amazing If with Helen, and I was able to explore the idea of consulting, something I'd always thought would be interesting as one of my values is variety and one of my strengths is strategic thinking. I also reflected on my stint leading a corporate responsibility team and decided to look into a role in a charity or social enterprise. Exploring these possibilities helped me realize that I wanted to move away from the large organizations where I'd spent most of my career into a smaller, fast-growing environment that would develop my skills in a different way.

I had so much fun exploring different options I found it hard to make a decision, but a mortgage and nursery fees soon reminded me it was time to make a choice! I chose to combine a few career possibilities, working part-time as a managing director for a small and fast-growing creative agency and spending the rest of my time focusing on Amazing If. Recently I returned to the Gather event which had kick-started my belief in career possibilities, this time as a mentor for the attendees. Sharing my experiences with people whose situation I had been in nine years ago, my advice was: ditch the plan, explore possibilities and you'll have a career that works for you.

Your career why

Future possibilities focus on what you want to do in the future and now we are going to move on to why you go to work every day. In his bestselling book, *Start With Why*, Simon Sinek talks about the value for organizations of starting with their 'why' rather than their 'what'. For example, Google's 'what' would be something along the lines of 'building the world's best search engine', but their 'why' is 'a way of organizing the world's data'. At Amazing If, our 'what' is 'to create impactful and actionable career content', but our 'why' is 'wouldn't it be amazing if we made work better for everyone?' Our 'whys' are more personal, emotional and compelling than our 'whats'. Everyone's 'why' is unique, and your approach to discovering your career 'why' will be personal to you. In this section we will share a couple of ideas for how you might do this.

Vision boards

A vision board is a visual representation of your 'why'. Vision boards are useful as they help us to visualize our ideas for the future into something tangible that you can draw inspiration from every day.

In summary, we need to see it, before we can believe it.

Before starting your vision board, it is useful to have your ideas from a couple of other exercises: your career must-haves and your values (Chapter

Three) and the possibilities you thought about earlier in this chapter. Use these to search for images that represent the things that are important to you, now and in the future. Your vision board should represent all aspects of your life, not only your goals for work.

> 'Before we can believe in a goal, we first must have an idea of what it looks like.'
>
> **FRANK NILES, SOCIAL SCIENTIST**

Some tips and things to consider as you create your vision board.

○ Select every image carefully. When designers put together mood boards for a concept or trend, every picture is carefully curated and considered. Apply the same care and attention to your pictures as each image should represent something that matters to you.

○ Your vision board can be physical or virtual, depending on what works best for you. Your board should be somewhere you'll see it regularly, like your screensaver on your phone, a Pinterest board or pinned up on a wall where you work.

○ Whether you share your vision board with anyone is entirely up to you. The purpose of a vision board is to motivate and inspire you and as long as it does that then it's doing its job.

○ Your vision board can change at any time. As your life twists and turns so will your vision board, with some things staying the same and others being replaced or evolving.

If you'd like some further inspiration for this exercise head to our resourcing section on amazingif.com to see an example of Helen's vision board.

Personal manifestos

If creating a vision board doesn't feel right for you, try writing a personal manifesto instead. Or you could have a go at both a vision board and a manifesto as they are complementary exercises and you might gain different insights from each method.

A good personal manifesto has three key elements:

1. It clearly communicates what is important to you: your beliefs, opinions, motives and intentions.
2. It is a source of inspiration and focus throughout your career.
3. It uses positive language that inspires action.

A good way to start your manifesto is to finish this sentence: 'Happiness is ...'

In the box below, capture any initial thoughts, words or ideas that sprang to mind as soon as you read that sentence.

☺ Happiness is _____

_____

_____

_____

_____

_____ ☺

Your manifesto can be words, paragraphs, stories, bullet points, whatever feels compelling for you. Once you've written your manifesto it's worth revisiting it every six months or so to see if anything has changed. When you get them right, personal manifestos remain relatively consistent as they reflect your view of how you want to live your life and what's important to you. Sarah first wrote her manifesto in 2012 and has changed it once since then, when her son Max was born.

SARAH'S PERSONAL MANIFESTO:
thinking, creating, learning

ACHIEVE:
Be ambitious, you can achieve more than you know.

LEARN:
Stay curious and always be a work in progress.

PEOPLE:
Spend time with people you care about, who care about
and inspire you, and who have a positive impact on your life.
Stick with the radiators and ditch the drains.

KNOW YOURSELF:
Focus on the things you're best at, enjoy and love what you do.
Know that your work matters to you and makes a
positive impact on others.

HAPPINESS IS:
Tom (partner), Max (when he sleeps) and close family/friends,
sport, developing and launching new enterprises, helping people
thrive in a squiggly career, the seaside, autumn, fiction,
cookies and a cup of tea.

Part Two –
Futureproofing Your Skills

Developing the core skills of strengths, values, confidence, networks and future possibilities will transform your ability to take ownership of your own career development. These skills will provide you with a strong foundation of self-reflection and action to build on throughout the rest of your career. Over the past few years we have spotted three 'up and coming' skills that we think are going to become more important at work, and these are: curiosity, feedback and grit. We have started to incorporate these into lots of our workshops and know that they are relevant and valuable for participants. In the spirit of squiggly careers, we have included our work-in-progress thinking, ideas and actions about these important skills so you can get ahead and make a start right now.

Future skill 1: Curiosity

One of Sarah's favourite interview questions to ask is: 'Can you share with me something you're curious to learn more about and why?' Lots of people find this a tough question to answer. Not because they're not good at what they do, quite the opposite. It is easy to become so focused on your own role and organization that you don't take the time to look up and see what's happening in the world. And yet staying curious is the key to spotting trends, opportunities, risks and managing complexity, all characteristics that are useful in a squiggly career.

> 'I think, at a child's birth, if a mother could ask a fairy godmother to endow it with the most useful gift, that gift would be curiosity.'
>
> **ELEANOR ROOSEVELT**

Dr Tomas Chamorro-Premuzic, psychologist and entrepreneur, argues that our ability to be curious is not determined by our IQ but instead by our CQ, our curiosity quotient.[25] People with a high CQ are inquisitive, open and generate original ideas. His research suggests if you have higher CQ you will deal with ambiguity more successfully, be able to translate complex problems into simple solutions and prioritize investing in your own development. Francesca Gino, a professor at Harvard Business School, also shares a compelling business case for curiosity. Her research shows that an organization that fosters curiosity in its employees benefits from fewer conflicts, inspires novel problem-solving and leads to better outcomes.[26]

Often it's hard to prioritize curiosity. We see it as a nice-to-do rather than an essential part of our jobs. Sometimes we don't put intentional effort into staying curious and expect it to happen as part of our day job. To help you combat this, we've shared three ideas on how to spark your curiosity and five ways that we each stay curious day to day.

> Staying curious takes intentional effort and we need to prioritize curiosity as an essential part of doing our jobs well.

Three ways to stay curious

1. Meerkat moments

Meerkats are famous for poking their heads up frequently to look around, spot danger and decide where to head to next. To us they typify curiosity. We encourage people to create 'meerkat moments' for themselves and the people they work with in a number of different ways. Building curiosity into your role and teams can be as simple as starting a Slack channel named #staycurious, holding meetings in different spaces such as a museum or exhibition, or scheduling a five-minute slot in a weekly meeting where someone volunteers to share something they have found inspiring from a different category of work or industry.

2. Figure out your curiosity profile

Harvard Business Review has a great free assessment called 'What's Your Curiosity Profile?' that you can take to work out what type of curiosity you exhibit most. You can find out what your curiosity profile is and see how your curiosity levels stack up compared to others in three areas – intellectual hunger, unconventionality or experiential curiosity. As a team at work, you could take this assessment and share your profiles in a team meeting. It would be interesting to partner with someone who has a different profile to you and discover how you both stay curious.

3. Curiosity crowdsourcing

Curiosity crowdsourcing is the name of a simple game we include as part of our workshops. It's designed to help you share and 'steal' curiosity from each other and works best in large groups, though it can also be used for smaller groups of people.

This is how it works:

○ Find a partner and share one way you stay curious at the moment (we typically do this with everyone standing up).

○ As a pair find another pair and all four of you share another way you stay curious.

○ Keep repeating this exercise until everyone in the room is in a large circle sharing one way they stay curious.

By the end of this exercise you will have lots of ideas for how you can stay curious. We've each shared five ways that we stay curious, so you can steal the ones you find intriguing for yourself …

Five ways Sarah stays curious

1. **Subscribe to Stack.** Stack is a magazine subscription service that sends you a different magazine each month. You never know what you're going to get so you end up reading magazines on everything from dog photography to Polish economics!

2. **One 'random' person rule.** I arrange to meet at least one person I don't know very well each month without a specific agenda or outcome for the meeting. Sometimes they are interesting chats that lead to collaborations and even on occasion to new friendships.

3. **Curiosity collaborators.** Find someone who also wants to make curiosity a habit and decide on something you're going to learn together. For example, on our Amazing If Instagram TV feed Helen and I do a monthly book review, where we both read the same book and share

with our community our favourite line of the book, the one thing we disagreed with and a thumbs up/down on whether we'd recommend it to others. Committing to this means I read a new book that I might not otherwise have picked.

4. **Find someone or something that has curiosity as a natural talent.** Some people and brands are ahead of the game when it comes to curiosity. A couple of my favourites that everyone can access are thecoolhunter.net, a global hub of creativity ranging from design to food, and do lectures.com, which describes itself as 'the encouragement network'. On their website you can find inspirational talks from passionate and creative people.

5. **Play with stuff.** The best way to learn about something in my experience is to have a go for yourself. I was intrigued to learn how chatbots worked, so in 2018 we began experimenting with creating a squiggly careers chatbot, which I hope will be on our website by the time you read this book. And if it isn't that's OK too, you learn as much from making mistakes and things not working as you do from getting them right. Our philosophy when playing with stuff is: done is better than perfect.

Five ways Helen stays curious

1. **Let YouTube be your guide.** Over the past few years, YouTube has become a significant destination to channel my curiosity towards. For example, when we started our Instagram channel I was curious about how we could build a community that adds value for other people. Spending time watching videos on YouTube and following recommendations about what to watch next provided me with lots of useful insights and tips about how to improve the types of content we were sharing and the questions we were asking our followers.

2. **Ask other people about podcasts.** Trying out new podcasts always stimulates my thinking. I love listening to different perspectives and ideas and I find it an efficient way to activate my curiosity as I fit it into my driving and commuting time. One of my favourite questions to ask people is what podcasts they listen to. It always gives me a deeper insight into people as well as picking up some new additions for my subscriptions.

3. **Talk to taxi drivers.** This always makes Sarah laugh. I will strike up a conversation with anyone. I love talking to taxi drivers and finding out about their life and experiences. They always have great stories and I often find they have led very squiggly careers. It doesn't just have to be taxi drivers though. I talk to people on trains, planes and in cafes! Obviously, I only do it when it feels appropriate and the other person looks open to talking, but I always feel energized by these random chats, fuelled by my interest in other people's lives.

4. **Curate curiosity with Feedly.** With so much to read and so many sources of inspiration, keeping up with the latest thinking can feel overwhelming. Feedly is a great app for curated curiosity. It's a free, simple app that means you can see all your news feeds in one place. You can sort sites into topical categories, watch YouTube videos (handy for my first point) and read articles without any adverts. It cuts down on opening lots of different emails and trawling websites and means I can be more focused about the things I want to read in depth. It also opens my eyes to things I might otherwise have missed.

5. **Try out new apps.** I'm a bit of a tech geek at heart and love to try out new apps. I stay curious by looking in magazines and at Apple's App of the Day for recommendations and then download them and have a play with them. They don't always stick with me as part of my daily habits, but just using them often helps me to think more creatively and come up with new ideas.

How are you going to stay curious?

Now that we've shared our ideas on staying curious, it's time for you to think a little bit more about what you're interested in staying curious about and how you're going to do it.

Five ways I will stay curious today
In the box opposite, write five ways you are going to stay curious.

_____

Now think of one way you could help your team at work be more curious.

_____

Future skill 2: Feedback

Feedback is a gift ... in theory. As researchers Gretchen
Spreitzer and Christine Porath showed in their 2012
study, one of the best ways to help employees thrive is
to give them feedback.[27] Feedback creates opportunities
to learn and provides people with energy. Importantly,
the research also showed that the quicker and more
direct the feedback, the more useful it is.

'Feedback is the
breakfast of champions.'

**KEN BLANCHARD,
AUTHOR & SPEAKER**

Barriers to feedback

Unfortunately, there are some significant barriers which get in the way of providing great feedback that is helpful for both individuals and organizations. When we run sessions on feedback, we ask people to write down all the words they associate with giving and receiving feedback and then to categorize those words into the percentage that are positive, neutral and negative. The results vary by group, but it is not uncommon to find over 50 per cent of the words in the negative bucket. Negative connotations around feedback get in the way of both asking for and delivering it. If you have received feedback in the past that has damaged your confidence it takes a lot of bravery to ask for it again as our brains are hardwired to protect us against threats.

Delivering feedback is a skill that most people don't receive training for or get the opportunity to regularly practise. A fear of upsetting someone leads to avoidance rather than action.

Squiggly careers add even more challenges into the mix. Remote working, organizations with multiple geographic locations, and project teams where you work with new people regularly are becoming the rule rather than the exception. When decreased face-to-face interaction, transient jobs and cross-cultural teams are the norm, our approach to feedback needs to reflect the environment we are working in if it is to have a positive impact.

Radical candour

Some organizations have embraced feedback in a completely new way, using an approach called radical candour, which Helen referred to in her story in Chapter Four: Confidence. The idea of radical candour has been popularized by high-profile adopters in Silicon Valley such as Facebook and Google. Kim Scott (the author of *Radical Candor*) defines the term as 'to care personally and challenge directly'. Her assertion is that the adoption of radical candour will deliver the best work of your lives and build the best relationships of your career.

Rob O'Donovan, co-founder of British start-up CharlieHR, has implemented radical candour throughout his organization. So, what does that mean in practice? Well, as an example, every Monday the team take an hour out of their day to sit down and share feedback. Rob leads from the front and there is a particular focus on sharing negative feedback. For example, he received feedback that his emails were long and unwieldy. He thanked everyone for letting him know and committed to being more concise in the future. He shared with us that, though it's not foolproof, when everyone is committed to the idea and the behaviour is modelled by the leaders of the organization, it can produce great results. Rob feels his team are quicker to spot and respond to problems when they arise and that deeper relationships are formed between team members. He was also, perhaps unsurprisingly, honest in his view that it doesn't work for everyone and that it is easy to let the level of candour reduce over time, so there is a consistent need to re-energize and remind everyone of why it's important.

How to deliver feedback

Relevant, real-time, regularly

Most people's experience of feedback tends to fall into one of two categories. One: feedback is given in a formal way as part of an appraisal or performance management process that happens once or twice a year. Two: feedback doesn't exist as a defined process in your organization, so a more informal approach is taken, which might mean you receive ad hoc feedback or no feedback at all. Neither of these approaches are ideal, as feedback works best when it is relevant to an individual's objectives, it is delivered in real-time and is shared regularly. We call relevance, real-time and regularity the three Rs of feedback – an easy way to remember how to incorporate feedback into your day-to-day work.

Relevant. If you are delivering feedback, make it as specific and personalized as possible. The more relevant the feedback is to the person receiving it, the more helpful it will be. For example, instead of telling someone you thought their presentation was great, tell them *why* the presentation was great:

I thought your presentation today had a really positive impact on the team. You made the content relatable to everyone and it felt like you cared personally about the topic.

It's even better if you can relate your feedback to someone's strengths or development areas:

I thought your presentation today had a really positive impact on the team. We've chatted before about how powerful storytelling can be to help influence and persuade people, and today I saw that in action. Keep going with this, it worked brilliantly.

Real-time. Feedback has the most impact when it is delivered as close to the activity it relates to as possible. You don't have to wait for a meeting with your manager or an official review conversation. If you give feedback straight after a project, meeting or presentation it is easier to be specific about what you observed, and it is also more helpful for the person receiving the feedback as they will be able to contribute their own self-reflections on how something went. And if there is a problem that needs fixing you have the chance to redeem the situation if you take action quickly.

Regularly. Feedback is easier to give and receive when it becomes a habit. If it is integrated into how you work then it starts to have the most impact for everyone. One of the advantages of radical candour is that it's integrated into an organization's culture and becomes part of 'how we do things around here'. Over the past few years Microsoft have adopted the philosophy of a growth mindset across their organization, including how their employees are encouraged to give and receive feedback, sharing their 'perspectives' through regular and scheduled 'connect' conversations. This creates a climate where regular feedback is expected and encouraged.

What went well / even better if

'What went well / even better if' is the technique we use to give each other feedback and how we ask participants in our workshops to share their thoughts with us. This technique has worked better than any of the others we've tried, for a few reasons. Language matters when it comes to feedback and the phrase 'even better if' is a positive way to offer people developmental feedback. In their 2004 article, academic Emily Heaphy and consultant Marcial Losada found that high-performing teams give each other more than five positive comments for every one criticism.[28] Using 'even better if' helps to phrase feedback with positive intent.

The simplicity of 'what went well / even better if' means that it can be used informally and quickly, using a WhatsApp or Slack message to share reflections after a team meeting for example. Many companies have started to take on this style of feedback. COOK is a food manufacturing retailer in the UK, which in 2019 was ranked fourteenth in the *Sunday Times* best companies to work for, and was the top-placed manufacturer. COOK was one of our first clients, and they quickly and successfully adopted our 'what went well / even better if' approach to feedback, across all aspects of their business. In their retail shops, 'what went well' includes points like welcoming people and making recommendations, and 'even better ifs' were the potential to get tasters out more quickly and improve product knowledge on new brands. In their kitchens 'what went wells' were focused on areas such as successful delivery of the production plan or three new dishes made efficiently, and 'even better ifs' included areas for improvement such as remembering to leave enough time for cleaning at the end of a shift.

Situation, result, impact

An alternative to 'what worked well / even better if' is a model called SRI, standing for situation, result, impact. This is a useful tool for providing structured feedback, particularly if you are providing someone with difficult feedback, as it helps you to be objective.

For example:

Last week when you were asked to contribute to a new project (situation) you responded in a way which was perceived to be defensive and unhelpful (result) and this means that people are concerned that you are not interested in contributing to the wider team success outside of your individual role (impact).

Using this structure in advance can help you to both prepare the content for a discussion and to feel comfortable in the delivery of your message. This will create a better environment for the conversation with the person you are delivering the feedback to.

Reflect on how effective your feedback is by considering these questions

1. When was the last time you gave someone only positive feedback?

2. When was the last time you asked for feedback?

3. Are you giving yourself feedback weekly on 'what went well' and 'even better if'?

Future skill 3: Grit

'Grit is living life like it's a marathon, not a sprint.'

DR ANGELA LEE DUCKWORTH

Angela Duckworth is the go-to guru on grit, the sustained application of effort towards a long-term goal. Her research into who is successful and why, as outlined in her book *Grit*, found that skill isn't just something you are born with, it's a result of talent multiplied by the amount of effort that you put into it. And, when it comes to achievement, it's effort again that makes the difference. Effort, and therefore grit, matters twice as much as any natural talent:

Talent x *effort* = skill
Skill x *effort* = achievement

On the topic of effort, it's worth briefly referencing the famed '10,000-hour rule', popularized by Malcolm Gladwell in his book *Outliers*. The simplified version of the rule suggests that people who reach peak performance, from athletes to musicians, have practised for 10,000 hours to reach that point. In fact, the original research conducted by Anders Ericsson and Robert Pool demonstrated the importance of something called deliberate practice. Deliberate practice is being honest with yourself about what you want to improve, finding the best way to achieve that improvement and then making that practice happen even if it is challenging and uncomfortable. Ericsson and Pool's research, shared in their book *Peak: How We Can All Achieve Extraordinary Things*, shows that people have an incredible capacity to improve, if we train in the right way. And the more time you dedicate to deliberate practice the better you will get, with the only limit on how far you can progress being yourself.

> As our careers become squigglier, deciding what we want to apply effort to is an important choice. What do you want to spend time deliberately practising and why?

Frequent role transitions and even complete career changes increase the value of transferable rather than role-specific skills. Whatever you choose to focus on, grit is what will translate skill into achievement. The great news is that we can all grow how gritty we are and here are some ways you can get started:

1. **Be fascinated by what you do.** Make sure you are working on answering the questions that fascinate you. A great example of this is Maria Popova, the creator of Brain Pickings, a website that reflects her fascination about what it means 'to live a decent, substantive and rewarding life'. Maria has maintained Brain Pickings as an ad-free website for over ten years and is solely funded by the donations from her readers. Ask yourself the question 'what am I fascinated by?' and make sure you allow yourself the time to explore it.

2. **Improve every day.** Strive to be better today than you were yesterday. It's important to take time to think about what you are grateful for and what you're doing well. But it's also good to reflect on what you could be doing better. Journaling can be a good way to measure both how grateful you are and what you could be improving. In the last few years, gratitude journaling has become really popular. You could take this practice and use it to write down one idea for how you are going to be better the next day. Hopefully at the end of each day you can cross the action from the day before off the list. Remember, no one is perfect so don't worry if you don't complete an action. You might choose to

roll it over to the next day or circle it as a way to remind yourself it is one you might use again in the future.

3. **Greater purpose.** The people who have grit recognize that their goals are contributing to a more significant goal beyond themselves. An inspiring example is the entrepreneur David Hieatt who founded Howies outdoor clothing, Hiut Denim and Do Lectures. His purpose was not only to create financially successful businesses but to do it in a way that created prosperity for a community in Wales that had suffered as a result of global outsourcing. He also created an initiative in Do Lectures to kick-start 200 businesses that make the world a nicer place.

    Purpose is discussed frequently in the context of modern careers, and it can feel like there is pressure to have a purpose that is contributing to a societal or charitable cause. Greater purpose is about understanding the relationship between your professional goals and the bigger goals that you are committed to achieving. This could be an organizational goal or an industry goal, or it might relate to a broader country-wide or even global goal. To identify your greater purpose start by connecting together two things, why you do what you do and why your organization exists.

4. **Growth mindset.** The grittiest people understand that the brain has plasticity and that no matter how much experience and success we have had we can always learn more. Satya Nadella, the CEO of Microsoft, has made growth mindset a significant part of his development and of the company's resurgence and success. Even as CEO of one of the world's largest companies he says: 'I need to be able to walk out and say, "Where was I too closed-minded, or where did I not show the right kind of attitude of growth in my own mind?"'[29]

Grow your grit

Reflect on how confident you are in each of the four areas we've just described and score yourself either low, low/medium, medium, medium/high or high. Then for every area write down one idea that will help you progress further up the scale. We've given an example for each to get you started.

Fascination in what you do

Low	Low/Med	Medium	Med/High	High

$\longleftarrow$ ———————————————————— $\longrightarrow$

Idea: ——————————————————————————————

——————————————————————————————

Example: write down one question that intrigues and fascinates you about the work that you do. Another way to think about this would be to address a problem you would love to solve.

Improve every day

Low	Low/Med	Medium	Med/High	High

$\longleftarrow$ ———————————————————— $\longrightarrow$

Idea: ——————————————————————————————

——————————————————————————————

Example: complete an eight-day learning log (include a weekend). At the end of every day write down one thing you have learnt that day, and one thing you'd like to improve for the next day.

Greater purpose

Low	Low/Med	Medium	Med/High	High

$\longleftarrow$ ———————————————————— $\longrightarrow$

Idea: ——————————————————————————————

——————————————————————————————

Example: divide a piece of paper into two columns. In one column write down all the reasons you go to work every day and keep going until you run out of ideas. In the second column list all the reasons why your organization exists. Can you draw a line to connect any of the thoughts across the two columns? For example, one of the reasons Sarah goes to work is to develop new ideas and the creative agency she works in exists to create ideas people want to spend time with, so that's a natural connection.

Growth mindset

| Low | Low/Med | Medium | Med/High | High |

Idea: _____

_____

Example: over the course of a week, spot the moments where you don't display a growth mindset and reflect on how you react when faced with a problem. Do you become defensive, angry, quiet, dismissive, despondent? Each time you feel this way, transition your mindset back to growth mode by asking yourself the question: what can I learn from this situation?

Futureproofing you

You've now spent some time thinking about your curiosity, feedback and grit skillset. We think these skills are only going to become more important in our careers, so by taking action now you will open up more opportunities for success and exploring interesting possibilities in the future. And, as we'll discuss in the next chapter, you don't need to develop every skill simultaneously and at the same pace. You can choose what feels most important for you to prioritize at the moment and start taking small steps straight away. What is critical is that you don't dismiss future skills as something to be worried about in the future. If you wait until you want to change jobs, or even careers, before you start thinking about the skills we've talked about in this chapter, it will take you much longer to make the transition you're hoping for.

Invest time, energy and effort in your future now and you'll be amazed by how many interesting career opportunities emerge over the course of your career.

Future possibilities: summary

1 The three-stage life of education > work > retirement is being replaced by a multi-stage, multi-transition squiggly career.

2 Ditch your career plan in favour of exploring future possibilities.

3 Define your obvious, ambitious, dream and pivot possibilities.

4 To discover more about a possibility be specific about what you need to know and who can help you.

5 Future possibilities focus on your 'what', career visions focus on your 'why'.

6 Use a vision board or personal manifesto to create a compelling and motivating statement of what is important to you in life and your goals for the future.

7 Treat yourself as a work in progress to futureproof your career skillset.

8 People with a high curiosity quotient (CQ) are more able to deal with ambiguity, solve complex problems with novel and simple solutions and deliver better outcomes for their organizations.

9 Feedback should be regular, real-time and relevant. On average people need five times more positive than developmental feedback. Use 'what went well / even better if' as a simple way to structure feedback.

10 Grit is more important than talent as an indicator of success. Grow your grit by being fascinated by what you do, improve each day, contribute to something bigger than yourself and adopt a growth mindset.

'The secret of getting
ahead is getting
started.'

MARK TWAIN

Summary
Embracing the squiggle

The five skills summary

Before we move on to the final two chapters, Career Conundrums and 100 Pieces of Career Advice, here's a reminder of the key things you've learnt about the five essential squiggly career skills over the course of the book so far.

You started your squiggly career journey by focusing on your super strengths in Chapter Two. Knowing what you're great at will help you enjoy your work, attract interesting opportunities and be part of more productive teams. In this chapter you worked through a four-step process to help discover your strengths and understand how to make them show up and stand out at work.

In Chapter Three you learnt about values. Your values are the things that motivate and drive you, they are what make you 'you'. Knowing your values means you can be yourself at work, improve your decision-making and helps you to build empathy for others. Discovering your values takes time, so we provided you with the tools to get started today by reflecting, spotting, scanning, prioritizing and defining the things that are important to you at work.

In Chapter Four we went deeper into confidence, and how to build belief in yourself, resilience and the ability to bounce back. You identified and drew your confidence gremlins, the things that hold you back from doing what matters to you, and came up with actions to cage the gremlins and stop them getting in your way. We discussed the importance of reflecting on your successes and developing a strong support system. We finished with some confidence boosting 'in the moment' hints and tips on watching your words, practising what you preach and staying calm.

In Chapter Five we focused on networking, which we define as 'people helping people'. We think the secret to unlocking the power of networking is to focus on what you can give rather than gain, something we describe as 'career karma'. Having a strong network means you can develop meaningful relationships, access diverse perspectives and build awareness of your personal brand. We covered tools to help you assess your network and make sure you are discerning, deliberate and diverse in your approach to building your relationships.

Finally, in Chapter Six we went into the future! Career plans and destinations are disappearing, and they've been replaced by exploring future possibilities. You identified four possibilities (obvious, ambitious, dream and pivot) that you can start taking action on today. We finished the chapter with three 'up and coming' career skills – curiosity, feedback and grit – that we think are worth starting to invest your time and energy in now to futureproof your career.

Start small, scribble, share and keep going

By the time you've reached this point, we hope you have a book full of scribbled notes, folded down corners and pages full of actions ready to leap into life. Knowing and using your strengths, living your values, caging your confidence gremlins, building a network and exploring your future possibilities are all instrumental skills that will help you realize the promise of this book: ditch the ladder, discover opportunity and design a career that works for you.

Squiggly careers are full of opportunity, and with the proactive application of the tools and advice we have shared you can craft a career that makes you happy, fulfilled and successful (whatever that means to you). Work is such a significant part of our lives that we should take every opportunity we can to make it the best that it can be.

Before we end with our Career Conundrums and 100 Pieces of Career Advice chapters, we have three final recommendations to help you develop your squiggly career skills.

1. **Start and never stop**

   The tools and advice in the book can help you at all stages of your career. Come back to them often. Redo the exercises and reflect on what has changed. You never stop learning and you will be able to gain and apply new insights as you and your career grow and develop.

   You have kick-started your self-awareness and development muscles. To stay in shape you need to keep training and practising to stay 'career fit'.

2. **Share the tools with others**

   The more you practise our exercises and tools, the more familiar, present and useful they will be in your career. Additionally, you can use them to help other people understand how they can be their best at work and make a positive difference to their future.

3. **Take action now**

   Each of the exercises in this book encourages you to take action on your reflections. Sometimes our own development ends up at the bottom of our to-do list. It is something we all mean to do and want to do, but somehow other things always seem to get in the way. However, no one cares about your career as much as you do. You need to take action now because you own your future. Once you make a start, it becomes much easier to build momentum and spark positive change.

   Take an action today, no matter how small. You will never regret investing in yourself and your career.

Staying connected in your squiggly career

It's important to share your career development with people who will help you along the way. There are lots of ways we, and the community that we've built online, can continue to support you beyond this book. We'd love to hear how this book has helped you, and answer any questions that you might still have.

Here's a reminder of how you can get in touch:

Email us directly at: helenandsarah@amazingif.com.

Or stay connected to squiggly career conversations and resources in three places:

Instagram: @amazingif
Follow our page to get access to daily career tips and tools, and join our community of squiggly careerists.

Podcast: *Squiggly Careers*
Listen to weekly episodes that offer actionable insights on a range of career topics and hear from thought-provoking expert guests sharing their wisdom once a month.

Website: www.amazingif.com
Find articles and online courses that will continue your career development.

Finally, we hope you have a very happy squiggly career!

PS. Turn the page to discover how to tackle the most common career conundrums people face and be inspired by Chapter Eight: 100 Pieces of Career Advice. You'll find some useful tips and insightful wisdom in these sections for you, your friends and colleagues.

Chapter 7
Squiggly Career Conundrums

Through training, managing and coaching people, we have observed common career conundrums that impact most people at work today, regardless of age, seniority, role, industry, gender or geography. In this chapter we cover the seven conundrums we are asked about most frequently, sharing our insights and ideas on the action you can take. Some of the questions have been prompted by the squiggly nature of careers today, such as 'should I start a side project?' Other conundrums have always been relevant to work, such as 'how to achieve work/life balance' – but although the questions may be familiar, the answers have evolved to reflect the fast-changing nature of work.

We answer each conundrum by sharing a mixture of research and our personal perspectives and experiences. Many of the conundrums relate to earlier chapters of the book, and we've signposted these at the end of each section. We've also included ideas on what else you can read, watch and listen to if you want to dig a little deeper into the subject.

In case you want to dive straight into the conundrum that feels most pressing for you right now, turn the page to see the seven we've included.

1. Should I start a side project? p.167

2. How do I find a mentor? p.172

3. What should I do if my organization doesn't invest in training? p.178

4. How do I achieve work/life balance? p.182

5. Should I stay or should I go? p.188

6. How do I build my personal brand? p.192

7. How do I demonstrate I'm a leader when I don't have a team? p.196

1 Should I start a side project?

Let's start with what a side project is. A side project or side hustle is a project that you work on outside of your primary job (which is the work you do to ensure you can pay the bills). Over the past few years it has become fashionable to have one or even a few projects on the go in addition to your main work. You can spot this trend in the way that people are describing their jobs now. The traditional job title description is being replaced by multiple descriptions, e.g. marketer/writer/fundraiser, or copywriter/musician/street-food aficionado. In many ways, having plural roles is not a new thing. Leonardo da Vinci, to take a classic example, had many strings to his bow: architect, artist, musician, mathematician, inventor, engineer. But the increased awareness, openness and publicity of side projects, and the freedom they afford to the modern worker, is prompting more and more people to ask the question: 'Should I start a side project?'

Side projects come in many shapes and sizes and are driven by different personal motivations. There are a few common reasons why people start a side project and they tend to be trying to solve a problem or testing a new business idea. In our experience, there is always personal passion connected to the project as well. Before you start a side project ask yourself: 'Why am I starting this project? What is my motivation?' To bring this to life further, in this section we have shared a few examples of real side projects that all had different starting points. If you have already decided a side project is for you, or you already have a side project on the go, skip ahead to the second part of this section where we share five ways to supercharge your side project.

Passion side projects

Projects that sit in this category tend to be the closest to what could be described as a hobby. They give you the opportunity to spend time on something you are personally passionate about and that is usually unrelated to your current day job. These projects are rarely driven by financial gain and there may be no clear outcome other than to experiment and play. For example, a person we have worked with, Hannah, is writing a book where the concept is the book grows older as you do. The book tells the same story from a number of different perspectives: a five-year-old girl, a teenager and then a woman in her thirties. For Hannah, a strategist in her day job, the book gives her a focused way of writing creatively and has the added benefit of being something she finds therapeutic.

Problem-solving side projects

Sometimes side projects grow out of solving a problem or spotting a gap in the market where a need isn't being met.

Annaliese, one of our workshop attendees who works in HR, shared her problem-solving side-project story with us:

> When I was planning my wedding and various friends' hen parties, I could never find the personalized items I wanted. This year (2018), after meeting Amazing If, I stopped making the excuse that I didn't have time, bought a machine that cuts unique patterns and pictures for crafting, using my Freedom Pot,* and started my side project. I have more energy as I'm excited to get home and get creating. And only six months in I can already see the benefits of having a side project. I feel more creative, am learning more about social media and how to organize my time, as well as benefitting from a little extra income.

* The Freedom Pot is a training fund provided by the company Annaliese works for (MoneySupermarket Group), where employees can choose how to spend the money as long as it relates to their development. An amazing initiative!

Idea-testing side projects

There are some side projects that are started with the intention of testing an idea to see if it could be a feasible business. This is a smart, low-risk way of seeing if a business idea you've imagined works in reality. This testing is particularly important as 42 per cent of start-ups cite a lack of need for their product or service as the reason they don't succeed.[30] These projects, unless they are charitable, are usually intended to make money at some stage. Kindeo, an app created for families to share and store their stories in one place online, has been developed in this way. Seb Royce, one of the co-founders, continues to hold a day job as Executive Creative Director at an advertising agency, as the business develops their proposition. There are a number of now famous and successful businesses that started in this way, including Slack, WeWork, Twitter, Groupon and Instagram.

> Side projects give you the chance to learn, meet new people and pursue your passions.

Supercharge your side project

To supercharge your side project we have suggested five top tips from our own experience of running side projects for over ten years as well as from other 'side-projecters' we know.

1. Start

Done is better than perfect when it comes to side projects. Remember, this is your opportunity to try stuff out without the constraints of your day job getting in the way. This sounds easy but the reality can feel hard at times. You know that you could improve something if only you had more time, money or expertise, and that can lead to procrastination and never quite hitting the 'go' button. The reality is that the best way to learn and improve is to get started. One of the benefits of starting a side project is that it will teach you the power of prioritizing as you juggle your work commitments with the project. Action should win out over perfection in the majority of cases when you are prioritizing your side-project to-do list.

2. **Collaborate**

There are a number of benefits to collaborating with other people on your side project. You can share the workload, expand your network and connect with people who share the same passion as you. Solo side projects are, of course, always an option as you might have a personal passion or idea you want to explore for yourself; if this is the case, find out what communities exist physically or virtually that you would benefit from being part of. Stephanie Broadribb is a professional career coach and also a crime-fiction writer. Writing can be quite a solitary endeavour so to stay connected she collaborates with other writers to run creative writing workshops in prisons across the UK.

3. **Share**

Share your side project with as many people as possible, as you never know who might be able to help you. Talking about your projects will give you confidence in explaining the ideas to others, and it will make you more interesting to chat to as your passion for the project will shine through. If relevant, add your side projects to your CV and online profiles like LinkedIn and The Dots.

4. **Learn and leapfrog**

Use each side project as an opportunity to learn about yourself: what you love working on, what you find frustrating, what you commit to and what gets in your way. These things all contribute to your self-awareness 'bank' and you can apply them across all aspects of your squiggly career, not just your side projects. And see each new side project as a leapfrog from the previous one – even if it was a disaster, take what you have learnt about what not to do and move on to the next thing.

5. **Have fun**

If you are not enjoying your side project then there's a problem. These projects are opportunities to apply your strengths and live your values outside of work. If at any point it's not fun or is bringing you too much stress, stop and move on to the next thing. Life is too short not to enjoy your side project!

Learn more

○ From us: revisit Chapter Three: Values and listen to *Squiggly Careers* podcast, episode 31: 'How to Start a Side Project'.

○ One book to read: *Do/Fly: Find Your Way. Make a Living. Be Your Best Self* by Gavin Strange.

○ One video to watch: Tina Roth Eisenberg, 'Don't Complain, Create' (Vimeo).

○ One account to follow: @emmagannon (Instagram).

2 How do I find a mentor?

In Chapter Five: Networks, we discussed the importance of building relationships with people who can support your career development. Some of these people are likely to be mentors. We define a mentor as 'someone who provides you with insight, advice and ideas that help you to learn and grow'. Mentors are often credited with playing a pivotal role in supporting a successful career. As Lailah Gifty Akita, the Ghanaian founder of Smart Youth Volunteers Foundation says, 'Every great achiever is inspired by a great mentor.' People often get stuck on how to find the right mentor and start a mentor relationship. In answering this conundrum we'll start by addressing some mentoring myths that might be getting in your way, before focusing on three questions that will help you find a mentor and finishing with specific examples of how to ask for one.

Five mentoring myths

Myth 1: Mentors should be as senior as possible

If a mentor is 'someone who provides you with insight, advice and ideas that help you to learn and grow', it doesn't necessarily equal a more senior person. And in the context of a squiggly career, limiting yourself to only one type of mentor will reduce the impact mentoring can have on your career development. Organizations are starting to proactively recognize this with reverse-mentoring programmes. This is where typically younger employees mentor older, more experienced employees in areas where they have unique insights such as digital expertise or diversity and inclusion. And you don't need an organizational programme to spot opportunities for different types of mentoring. We were recently training a group where one participant had exceptional presentation skills developed in a previous career as a teacher. Her manager recognized this and asked her to mentor her on presenting, as it was an area she wanted to improve in.

Myth 2: Mentors are long-term relationships

Effective mentoring relationships can range from a one-off conversation over the phone to an indefinite 'always there' style of relationship. In a squiggly career it is likely that the number of mentors we have over our careers will increase, as will the number of short-term relationships. If we are changing roles, industries and even careers more frequently, it makes sense that at least some of our mentoring relationships need to change to reflect the new context we are working in. The general rule is that mentoring relationships should be maintained for as long as they are valuable for everyone involved.

Myth 3: No one will be interested in mentoring me

Networking is 'people helping people', and typically people really enjoy and value the opportunity to help others. In a mentoring relationship it is common to feel concerned that as the mentee you are the one receiving all the value and not offering anything in return. However, when we speak to mentors, they will often share how a mentoring session is their favourite part of the week. If you haven't mentored anyone before, we would definitely encourage you to give it a go. Becoming a mentor, in any capacity, will help you to appreciate first-hand how much value you gain from the relationship, whether you are the mentor or the mentee.

Myth 4: You have to 'ask' for a mentor

Mentoring can sound formal and come with an implication of a significant time commitment. When you are approaching someone for a mentoring conversation there is no obligation to ask, 'Will you be my mentor?' In fact, we would recommend that you do not take this approach. Instead, ask if someone can spare the time for a short chat over the phone or in person on a specific topic you are looking for some insights on. This approach tends to work better for a few reasons: you have made a request that is easier to say yes to, as it is low-commitment and flexible; it is also easier to say yes if someone has been clear about what help they need. If the person you have contacted doesn't feel able to help, they will often recommend someone else in their place. This approach also gives you a chance to have an informal 'chemistry' meeting. There are some people you will 'click' with and these are the people most likely to be your long-term mentors. With other people you might have an impactful one-off conversation, and that is still a successful mentoring conversation.

Myth 5: You need to know your mentors

The advantage of a one-to-one mentoring relationship is that the advice and ideas you receive will be personalized to you and your specific context, opportunities and challenges. However, technology means that we now have access to a wider range of inspiring people whom we may never meet but who are still useful in helping us learn and grow in our careers. We call these people 'distance-learning mentors'. It is a useful exercise to identify one or two distance-learning mentors and dedicate time to exploring their work. One of Sarah's distance-learning mentors is Roman Krznaric, a social philosopher. She hasn't met Roman, but she invests time in learning from his latest thinking, whether that is visiting his pop-up Empathy Museum or re-reading his books *Carpe Diem Regained* and *The Wonder Box*. We would recommend that the majority of your mentors are people you know and that you complement these with one or two specific distance-learning mentors as it will bring new thinking and perspectives to your development.

How to find a mentor: *three (self-reflection) questions*

Spend some time reflecting on what mentoring you are looking for and why. This will make it much easier to find and ask for a mentor in a way that feels authentic to you.

The three questions to focus on are:

1. What do I want to learn and why?
2. Who do I already know who could help me or could connect me to someone else who can?

3. How can I ask for mentoring in a way that is both interesting and authentic to me?

There are no right answers to these questions, it will depend on what you need support with, now and in the future.

Examples of how to ask someone for mentoring support

When asking for a mentoring conversation you are usually faced with one of two scenarios: you are being connected by someone you know, or you are effectively 'cold calling' someone. We suggest you adjust your approach to reflect the scenario. To bring this to life we have included an example for each below.

> Rather than asking for a mentor, start by asking yourself, 'What do I want to learn and why?'

Approach with no connection

The key here is to communicate that you have an understanding of and an appreciation for their work. Without this, connection requests can come across as lazy or random. Here is an example of a considered approach:

> *I read your article on gravitas which you kindly shared on LinkedIn and your point on understanding your breathing really resonated with me. I have always struggled with feeling confident when speaking in front of large groups of people, but it is something I want to get better at as I am passionate about sharing my work on children's development. I was wondering if you could spare half an hour to chat to me about any other hints and tips you could share on this topic. If you don't have the time at the moment then no problem; if there is anyone else you could recommend I get in touch with or any suggestions for what I could read, watch or listen to, I am very open to ideas. Thanks very much, Rachel.*

Approach with connection

It may have been a while since you connected with this person, so remind them of the last time you spoke or the reason you both connected originally. Demonstrate a knowledge of the individual and their context in your message, for example:

> *Hi Gareth, Katherine Waters kindly introduced us as she felt you might be able to help me with a career transition I'm currently exploring. I'm working in IT at present, and am hoping to move into my first leadership position with my next career move. I know you have done something similar recently and I would appreciate any insights you could share with me about your experiences. I'm in London regularly so could come to your offices at a time that suited you. I appreciate you will have lots on, having recently started your new role, so if now isn't the best time that's not a problem. I've attached my current CV as I thought this might be useful for you ahead of us catching up. Hope to meet up soon. Thanks very much, Henry.*

And one final tip … If someone says no

As we touched upon in Chapter Five on networking, if you don't get a response to your request or if someone says no, don't take it personally. There are lots of reasons why this might happen. Someone could be in the middle of a stressful period in their personal lives, caught up in a work project that requires 100 per cent of their focus and energy, not feel confident in their mentoring skills or already have a number of mentoring commitments … the list goes on. Don't feel disheartened. All of these variables are outside your control. What is in your control is what you decide to do next. There is rarely only one person who could provide you with the support you are looking for. And if you are getting lots of 'nos' or 'no responses', can you change your approach? Pip Jamieson, founder of tech business The Dots, asked a number of female tech founders for mentoring and struggled to get any traction. She realized that there are so few female tech founders that they get bombarded with requests for support, so she switched her focus and started asking male founders who she knew had daughters, and it worked. She received amazing support from some very high-profile male mentors.

Learn more

○ From us: revisit Chapter Five: Networks and listen to *Squiggly Careers* podcast, episode 18: 'How to Find a Mentor'.

○ One book to read: *Forget a Mentor, Find a Sponsor: The New Way to Fast-Track Your Career* by Sylvia Ann Hewlett.

○ One video to watch: Tanya Menon, 'The secret to great opportunities? The person you haven't met yet' (TED Talk).

○ One account to follow: @adamgrant (Instagram).

3 What should I do if my organization doesn't invest in training?

An IBM study revealed that employees who do not feel they are developing in a company are twelve times more likely to leave it.[31] We understand that it can feel frustrating if an organization is not prepared to invest in a training opportunity that you know would benefit both you and them. The unfortunate reality is that not all companies are great at supporting your learning, and you may at some point be denied access to training that would help your career and performance. Small organizations have to make tough choices about where to invest their often-limited discretionary funds. Large organizations may prioritize investing in learning that will benefit as much of the workforce as possible over individual learning requests.

We speak to thousands of people every year who share their squiggly career stories with us, and the people who are happy and succeeding are the ones taking ownership for their own career development. Of course, everyone hopes that their manager and organization will support their development, but it's important that you don't rely on other people to do the hard work for you. You need to be clear about what you want to learn and how you are going to make it happen. Sometimes this is easier said than done, so we've compiled three actions that you can start taking straight away to fuel your growth.

Action 1: Apply for grants, awards or bursaries that could help fund or partially fund your learning

Money is a barrier to some learning, both for organizations and individuals. However, across most industries there are opportunities to apply for awards or grants that can help fund your learning. If you aren't aware of any, ask around your network and seek out people who have undertaken similar learning to understand how they funded a particular programme. You might be positively surprised by how many opportunities are out there once you start looking. When you find the right resource, share your plan with your manager and organization, as early as possible. This gives everyone involved as much time as possible to consider if they are able to support you. Even if your organization is not in a position to support you financially, they might be willing to offer support in other ways, such as allowing you time off to study. And if your organization doesn't provide support, you have demonstrated that you value learning and curiosity and have the drive to make things happen. These are all qualities that most organizations value and want to retain, so you might end up realizing a different benefit to the one you were originally expecting, such as a secondment opportunity coming your way or even a promotion.

> Think creatively about all the ways in which your organization can support your learning beyond money. For example: time to study, project opportunities and mentoring.

Action 2: Create your own curriculum

Curating your own programme of learning is more accessible and feasible than ever before, thanks to the various technologies on offer today. With so much content, it can be hard to know where to start. Coursera, Skillshare, LinkedIn Learning and Udemy websites are good places to get some inspiration as they curate good-quality content into one place, either for free or at low cost. As you are creating your own curriculum think about two things: what you want to learn and how you learn best. Most of us benefit from at least some learning in an environment where there are other people to learn with and from. This doesn't necessarily need to be in person as many online courses now create communities of people who are learning together through things like live Q&As. This flexibility means you can continually adapt your curriculum, though we recommend you have between one and three learning objectives at any one point in time, otherwise you risk spreading your energy and time across too many things. Your learning objectives might be a mixture of personal and professional learning and your style of learning will vary based on both your personal preference and what you are learning.

Action 3: Become a learning advocate in your organization

If you would like your team, department or organization to change the way they invest in the learning and development of people, think about how you could become an advocate for this change. You can start small by sharing things you are learning that you think might be relevant to other people at work, which can be as simple as sending round an article or a summary of an event you attended. This is a brilliant opportunity to spend time with different people in your organization, to understand where they think the learning gaps are and what they think is getting in the way at the moment. By doing something like this you will often identify other people who are also advocates and are prepared to support you in driving change. Remember to start small. Don't try to solve all the organization's learning needs at once; pick the one that is the biggest priority and then suggest a trial or pilot so you can test and learn quickly. Once you have some momentum, more people will support you and it becomes easier to secure investment and expand further.

Learn more

○ From us: revisit Chapter Five: Networks and listen to *Squiggly Careers* podcast, episode 69: 'DIY Career Development'.
○ One book to read: *Mindset: Changing the Way You Think to Fulfil Your Potential* by Carol Dweck.
○ One video to watch: Crash Course channel (YouTube).
○ One account to follow: @farnamstreet (Instagram).

4 How do I achieve work/life balance?

This is probably the most common career conundrum we get asked about, and for good reason. The promise of a life where our work, health (physical and mental), family and spiritual needs are all in balance is a goal most people aspire to but many struggle to achieve.

There seems to be an endless and overwhelming stream of advice on how to tackle this conundrum, covering everything from minimizing distractions, working more productively, setting and sticking to boundaries, meditating to stay present and investing in your hobbies to fuel your happiness. Our view is that all these things can work, but they don't work for all of us, all of the time.

Creating some kind of 'work/life blueprint' that fits everyone is ineffective and distracts people from thinking through the really important questions about what 'good' looks like for them. Yes, science tells us that we need a minimum amount of sleep to be at our best (keep reading to find out the magic number), but beyond that, how you do your best work and what balance looks like for you is a question that requires personal reflection and action to achieve it. Even the word 'balance' might be something you need to consider. Its implication that we have metaphoric scales with work on one side and everything else on the other feels out of

> Everyone's version of balance is different, and it doesn't stay still. The best thing you can do is to take control of your choices to achieve the version of balance that works for you right now.

sync with today's reality and leads some people to create their own definition; for example, Sheryl Sandberg, COO of Facebook, prefers to use the term 'work/life integration'.

Our own learning is that balance is a moving beast and trying to be too rigid about it can cause frustration. We've been juggling side projects, motherhood, full-time roles and studying for many years and our version of balance has looked different for both of us throughout that time. It might not be other people's version of balance but that's fine, because what is most important to your happiness is that you make conscious decisions to spend time doing what you love. Using your personal insight to make informed choices gives you control over how you spend your time.

To get back control and find your own unique 'integration', you need to focus on two interrelated aspects:

○ **Feelings.** Knowing how you are doing in a particular moment: a day, week, month or year, and taking positive action to continue or change how you feel.

○ **Choice.** Having the self-awareness and confidence to make the right decisions for you, across all aspects of your life.

How are you feeling?

At the start of some workshops, we run an exercise where we ask everyone to anonymously answer the following question using one word: 'How is your life feeling at the moment?' We then ask everyone to repeat this exercise answering a subtly different question, again using one word: 'How would you like to describe your life at the moment?' Sometimes the words are similar or the same, which is brilliant. But more often than not, the two answers are quite different. People often describe their current state as: *stressed, anxious, frustrated, busy* and *frantic*. We even had the word *muddy* crop up in a recent session.

In contrast, the words that people often use to describe their desired state are *motivated, energized, inspired* and *happy*. The challenge is that people often feel unsure how to move from a negative to a positive feeling, or even worse, fear that it might not be possible. At its worst, this exercise shows that work is a huge source of stress rather than satisfaction in people's lives. But as we become more aware of the negative impact of stress in our lives, it becomes easier for us to tackle the problem.

Take a moment to reflect on these questions for yourself:

Using one word, how is your life feeling at the moment?

_____

Using one word, how would you like to describe your life at the moment?

_____

What choices are you making?

It is important to recognize that you have at least some control over how you spend your time. While work pressures or family demands may create challenges in the moment, over the long term it is your decisions and choices that will make the difference to how happy you feel about your work/life balance.

Think about your answers to the previous questions about how you are feeling right now. What are the choices you are currently making that are working for or against you? It might be that you're choosing to work in the evenings so you can feel prepared for the next day's meetings, but you're left feeling resentful that you haven't had a break from the 'day job'. Perhaps you are choosing to spend hours of your time each day scrolling through social media, but you are frustrated that you have no time to read a new book or learn a new skill. Or maybe you've made a commitment to leave your phone downstairs when you go to bed and it's helping you to feel more refreshed each day.

Write down your thoughts on the choices you are currently making that are impacting on your work/life balance, positively and negatively:

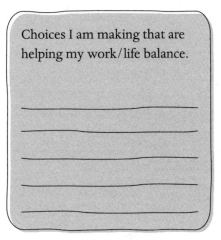

| Choices I am making that are not working for my work/life balance. | Choices I am making that are helping my work/life balance. |

With this insight, you can make a conscious decision to minimize the choices that are working against you. It's important to know that it may be hard to change all of your choices straight away, so we suggest starting with the one that you feel will be the most impactful in the short term. This will give you the motivation to keep going and make further improvements.

Choices that help you find balance

If you're struggling or would like some additional inspiration about choices that can help you to find your balance, we've listed five ideas that we think will be effective to get you started.

Choice 1: Get enough sleep

We all know sleep is important and the research is compelling. The brain needs seven to eight hours of sleep a night; any less and your concentration, creativity, mood regulation and productivity all take a hit.[32] The number of products designed to help us sleep better seems to have multiplied dramatically over the past few years, suggesting that we need more help than ever to wind down and sleep peacefully. We both have young children, a natural antidote to a good night's sleep, and so over recent years we have tried and tested a few tactics to get more rest. Reading Marie Kondo's book *Spark Joy* prompted us both to do a clear-out, and in particular to make our bedrooms as clutter-free as possible. Helen has moved her phone out of her bedroom to let her mind wind down. Sarah tries to exercise, even if it is just a thirty-minute walk every day, as she knows this will help her go to sleep quicker.

Choice 2: Exercise your mind and body

Walking is good for your brain and your body. Walking for just twelve
minutes will result in an increase in your attentiveness and self-confidence
and improve your creativity by an average of 60 per cent as exercise sparks
connections between different brain cells.[33] One of our friends, Ian
Sanders, runs a programme called Fuel Safaris, which offers walking
coaching sessions. Ian has found that walking while coaching means that
his participants are more open, able to solve problems and committed to
taking action. The choice to host walking meetings might help you to feel
more engaged and impactful in your work and make the hours you spend
there more meaningful to you.

Choice 3: Take a break

As Arianna Huffington pointed out in her open reply to Elon Musk's
declaration that he was working 120-hour weeks: 'People are not machines.
For machines – whether of the First or Fourth Industrial Revolution
variety – downtime is a bug: for humans, downtime is a feature. The
science is clear.' Everyone benefits from regular breaks, whether that is
taking the time to have a lunch break or a two-week holiday in the sun.
Technology is now an integral part of most people's lives, and at its best
makes life easier, but it also means that the ritual of leaving the office and
your work behind is disappearing, so you need to find new ways of doing
that for yourself. Most technology has the ability to be temporarily turned
off, and we can choose to turn off things like notifications that cause
unnecessary distractions. Bruce Daisley, author of *The Joy of Work*, reminds
us that by turning off notifications we will have more energy and creativity
at work. Daisley cites a study by Telefonica and Carnegie Mellon
University where participants were asked to turn off their notifications for
twenty-four hours to see what impact it had. Even after a day, people
reported an increase in productivity and concentration, and two years later
half the volunteers had opted to keep their notifications turned off.

Choice 4: Make a friend

Loneliness and isolation at work are becoming real problems. One study
suggests that 42 per cent of us don't have a single friend in the office.[34]
Hot-desking, multiple locations, varying hours and project work are all
becoming features of our careers and it is easy to see how this
environment could contribute to people feeling lonelier. The Hoxby

Collective, a company where all its members work virtually, encourages Hoxby meet-ups, where members living in the same area can choose to rotate working at each other's houses or in local coffee shops. This approach could be easily replicated by inviting someone to have lunch with you outside the office or sharing an event you're attending which is relevant to your job and asking whether anyone would like to join you.

Choice 5: Stop saying sorry

Have you ever made a decision to leave the office early to spend time doing something you love and felt guilty for it? Have you ever changed your working patterns and heard yourself say something along the lines of 'I'm really sorry, I can't make that meeting, I don't get in until 10 a.m. on a Thursday'? We find that a lot of people apologize for the choices they make about their work/life balance. This means they don't feel positive and empowered, instead they feel awkward and often default to old ways of working, conforming to norms rather than taking action that will help them to be their best.

If this feels like you, start becoming more conscious of how often you're apologizing for your choices at work. For example, how many times do you use the word 'sorry' every day, or each week? Be aware of whether certain people or situations trigger it and try to remove the apology from your communication. It might be that you have a hidden confidence gremlin here, so refer back to Chapter Four if you need some more help.

Learn more

- From us: revisit Chapter One: The Squiggly Career and listen to *Squiggly Careers* podcast, episode 39: 'How to Improve Your Work Well-Being'.
- One book to read: *Thrive: The Third Metric to Redefining Success and Creating a Happier Life* by Arianna Huffington.
- One video to watch: 'How to gain control of your free time' by Laura Vanderkam (TED Talk).
- One account to follow: @Headspace (Instagram).

5 Should I stay or should I go?

Whether or not to leave a role and move on to the next thing, either in your current organization or a new one, is often a difficult decision. Some of the previous 'rules' about how long to stay in a role or organization no longer apply as squiggly careers mean that we are all getting used to constant change. Even if you stay in the same role for a number of years, it's likely to evolve over time. There are a few questions we recommend asking yourself so you can make an informed decision about your next move.

Are you happy and learning?

Dame Cilla Snowball, ex-Group Chairman and Group Chief Executive of the UK's largest advertising agency and one of Sarah's long-term mentors, gave her some excellent advice about how to make a decision on whether or not to go for a new role. Ask yourself: are you happy and are you learning? As long as the answer is yes to both these questions then consider staying put. If one of those elements is missing, now might be the time to make a move. Cilla worked for Abbott Mead Vickers for twenty-six years, and says that the reason she stayed so long is that the answer to both these questions was always yes.

What's the job after the next job?

If you are considering your next move, think about what that role could lead to in turn. How does it help you continue to explore the career possibilities that are important to you? What new possibilities does it open up?

It is OK to take some time to think about a job offer; you shouldn't feel pressured into making a decision before you are ready. And it is OK to say no to a job if it is not right for you. It might not always feel like it but interviewing for a new role is intended to be a two-way process where you find out about the role and company and they find out about you. It is your decision whether a role is a good fit for you.

> When offered a job we become present-focused, sometimes to the detriment of remembering what we have learnt from the past and ignoring the implications for our future.

Will you use your strengths and live your values?

Beware the shiny objects when you are looking at your next move. Shiny objects, like job title, salary or office environment, can distract you from your career must-haves. On the surface they are alluring, and of course are not unimportant factors, but the appeal can be short lived if your day-to-day role doesn't give you the opportunity to apply your strengths and live your values. Once you have 'enough' money, increases in salary don't make us happier. Psychologist Daniel Kahneman and economist Angus Deaton from Princeton University showed that self-reported levels of well-being increase until we reach a salary of roughly US$75,000 (or £50,000) and after that increasing amounts of money had no further impact on happiness.[35] It's a clichéd phrase but in a squiggly career it is more important than ever to enjoy the journey rather than focus on the destination, as it is so hard to predict now what that destination is and indeed if there even is such a thing as a 'destination'.

Do you love your job, but not your manager?

Your manager has a significant impact on how much you enjoy your job. Research suggests that up to 70 per cent of someone's engagement in a role is determined by the person they work for.[36] A difficult relationship with a manager can often prompt people to think about moving roles. A job that you love isn't easily found so if you are enjoying your role but struggling with your manager see if you can improve the situation before making the leap elsewhere. Consider whether you have given the relationship enough time. As psychologist Bruce Tuckman identified in his work on high-performing teams, many relationships go through three phases of 'forming, storming and norming' before you reach the 'performing' phase where things will feel more in flow and comfortable. If you and your manager have different styles of work and different values, it can take even longer to reach a point where you both understand and appreciate each other.

The second thing to think about is giving your manager feedback about how you are feeling and the impact they are having on you. This can be intimidating, especially if you are not working in a natural feedback culture, but whatever the outcome of the conversation you will progress towards making a decision about whether you can make the relationship work or not.

Finally, consider whether you are running from your old role or towards a new one. It's important to be honest about the driving force behind your move. If you are running away from something in your current role – boredom, your manager, the culture, to give a few examples – it can affect the quality of your decision-making. When you are being pulled towards something because it excites you and aligns with your strengths and values, you're more likely to make a decision that will make you happier in the long term.

Learn more

○ From us: revisit Chapter Six: Future Possibilities and listen to *Squiggly Careers* podcast, episodes 28: 'How to Fix Your Career Plan', 57: 'How to Create a Vision for Your Career' and 70: 'Career Possibilities and the Radical Sabbatical'.

○ One book to read: *The Start-Up of You: Adapt to the Future, Invest in Yourself, and Transform Your Career* by Reid Hoffman and Ben Casnocha.

○ One video to watch: 'Why you will fail to have a great career' by Larry Smith (TED Talk).

○ One account to follow: @themuse (Instagram).

6 How do I build my personal brand?

It is useful to start by thinking about why brands exist. Brands are created as a way to help people choose between different products. The best brands are distinctive. They have attributes, features and benefits that you recognize, trust and feel good about buying. If you think about the brands that you feel the most connection to, these are often brands that you willingly recommend and advocate to others, as you feel confident in the product or service they provide. By buying and endorsing these brands you are also sharing with others something about yourself, what you stand for and believe in.

The principles of personal branding are pretty much the same as those for branding a product or service, it's just that your brand is you. In simple terms, personal branding is what you want to stand for.

Creating a strong personal brand will help you to have a successful squiggly career in a number of ways. Firstly, it means that interesting and relevant opportunities are more likely to find you, resulting in projects coming your way that you otherwise might not have known about. Secondly, other people will be able to confidently and accurately recommend you to others, growing your network as well as opening up new possibilities. Finally, if you build your personal brand in a way that is authentic, it will mean you are spending more time on the things that make you happy at work.

> Ask yourself the question: what do you want people to say about you when you're not in the room?

Technology means that our profiles are seen and shared in more places than ever before. Making sure that our brand is consistent in all the places we are visible and that it reflects what we want people to know about us has become increasingly important. Think about all of the places your brand shows up and audit them to make sure they are consistent in creating the impact you want to make.

Five personal brand principles

1. Start with your strengths and values

Your personal brand is built on your strengths and values. These are the things that are authentically and uniquely 'you' and provide the foundation for your personal brand. You don't need to be all things to all people. Decide on one or two areas that are true to you and which you feel passionate about. Think about what TED Talk you would do if asked or how you would describe yourself in one tweet.

2. Your personal brand is everywhere you are

Once you know what your personal brand is, explore and evaluate all the different ways in which you could bring this to life. Everywhere you are, virtual and physical, your personal brand goes with you. People who won't ever meet you in person are now in a position to have a point of view on your personal brand. Hopefully your main job gives you the opportunity to demonstrate your personal brand in action, and side projects can be a brilliant way of bringing your personal brand to life in different ways. Lauren Currie OBE is the Managing Director of NOBL in the UK, a global agency that helps leaders create change. Lauren is also the founder of #upfront, an organization dedicated to changing confidence, and while on maternity leave she and her husband set up the Letter Love Shop, which is a beautiful letter-art shop inspired by animals and nature. Before we even met Lauren, these projects had given us an insight into her personal brand. Our perception was we would meet someone who is entrepreneurial, creative and who 'walked the walk', as on her LinkedIn summary she describes her motto as 'doing not talking'. And when we met Lauren her impact in person matched our expectations. She was full of ideas and energy and genuine about her desire to make an impact in the areas she was passionate about.

3. Intent versus impact

One of the most useful ways to figure out if your intended personal brand is having impact on others is to ask someone you know how they would describe you to someone else (you can get a great insight into this when someone makes an introduction between you and another person). Another source of insight is good-quality LinkedIn recommendations. You can spot the LinkedIn recommendations that feel personalized as they are more specific than just saying someone is great to work with. And if you have a number of recommendations, you can look for common themes.

4. Win–win

Developing your personal brand should be good for you and your organization. Share what you want to stand for with your manager and peers in your organization. Other people in your organization will spot further opportunities to optimize your brand in ways that can benefit you and your organization. If your personal brand is not aligned with your current role or organization then this is where external activities such as side projects and volunteering can provide a useful stopgap in the short term. Ultimately, if what you stand for is in conflict with your job and/or organization this will make it difficult for you to build your personal brand effectively or for your organization to realize the benefit.

5. Always investing

Developing any successful brand takes time and continual investment. Your personal brand isn't something to tick off your to-do list. That's OK because if you are passionate about what you want to stand for then you will enjoy the process of building your brand as much as the positive outcomes along the way. Your personal brand is not set in stone. As your squiggly career develops so will your personal brand, and there may be moments where you want to pivot what you stand for. To kick-start taking action on your personal brand, set an objective to do one thing a week for the next six weeks to build your brand. It can be as simple as attending an event about a topic you're passionate about and then sharing what you learn with people at work, or figuring out three people who you think are doing amazing work in the area you're interested in and start to proactively follow, read, watch and listen to their work.

Learn more

○ From us: revisit Chapter Two: Super Strengths and listen to *Squiggly Careers* podcast, episode 25: 'Building Your Personal Brand'.

○ One book to read: *The Story Factor: Inspiration, Influence and Persuasion through the Art of Storytelling* by Annette Simmons.

○ One video to watch: 'How to Build Your Personal Brand in 2019' by Lavendaire (YouTube).

○ One account to follow: @ThisIsSethsBlog (Seth Godin, Twitter).

7 How do I demonstrate I'm a leader when I don't have a team?

The definition of what it means to be a leader is changing. Squiggly careers have been shaped in part by an evolving organizational environment where hierarchies are becoming flatter and there is a move away from the 'command and control' style of leadership popularized in the Industrial Revolution. Increasingly organizations are adopting more agile ways of working, based around projects and outcomes rather than an organizational chart. Some organizations are even experimenting with something called Holacracy, an approach where power is distributed throughout the organization, giving individuals and teams more freedom to self-manage, while staying aligned to an organization's purpose. There are over 1,000 organizations now exploring working in this way, and if you want to learn more, do some research into the American online shoe retailer, Zappos, as they have openly shared lots of their learning from working with this new style.

Leaders are defined by the skills they have, such as curiosity, resilience and adaptability, rather than their position on an organizational chart.

The most successful leaders we have worked with have a few things in common: they are self aware, they listen and stay curious. They also have the ability to influence and persuade, and they invest in their own learning and the development of others. The good news is that these are all skills that you can work on whether you are in an official leadership position or not. If you think laterally rather than literally about building your leadership capability, you can start to develop and demonstrate these skills now.

Lateral leadership ideas

Volunteering

Are there causes that you are passionate about and which could benefit from your strengths and give you the opportunity to develop your leadership skills? This could be in a formal capacity such as becoming a trustee for a charity or informally helping out with a fundraising event or coaching a local sports team.

Adopt a problem

What problems, big and small, are your team or organization facing that they could use some help on? These don't have to be big problems, they could be small niggles that no one has yet had the time or initiative to do anything about. These are great opportunities to show drive and the ability to make things happen, and give you the chance to work with a different group of people. Some examples of adopting a problem that we have seen people take on in the past include office moves, new company websites, organizing team events and leading team training.

Become a mentor

Think about who in your organization – an individual or a team – would benefit from understanding more about your skills and experiences. You don't have to wait to be asked to be a mentor, you can get in touch and ask if you can help in some way. You might volunteer to present at a future team meeting or offer an induction session to any new joiners in a team. And remember to share with your manager and HR team (if you have HR) that you would like to get some experience as a mentor and see if they know anyone whom they could connect you with.

Spot opportunities

Look for opportunities where you can get more exposure to and experience of leadership roles in your organization. If your manager is going away on holiday this could be a good opportunity to see if there is anything you could cover for him or her while they are away. Or if you know your manager is particularly busy with tight deadlines or an important project, could you offer to take on some of their other work temporarily? And this doesn't just apply to your manager, look out for opportunities with your peers too. This will help you develop a broader understanding of the work the team does, naturally improving your judgement and demonstrating your curiosity. As a leader you are often accountable for a number of different projects or areas simultaneously, so showing that you are flexible and adaptable is definitely an advantage.

Don't apologize

If you are interviewing for a role where you will be directly accountable for leading other people then answer honestly but don't apologize for your leadership experience to date. Focus on your strengths, why you are well suited for the role and share your lateral leadership examples. Think about what you could offer to a role that might be different to what more experienced leaders would bring, such as a fresh perspective, digital experience and a willingness to continually invest in your own development.

Learn more

- ○ From us: revisit Chapter Six: Future Possibilities and listen to *Squiggly Careers* podcast, episode 91: 'How to Manage for the First Time'.
- ○ One book to read: *Why Should Anyone Be Led by You? What It Takes to be an Authentic Leader* by Rob Goffee and Gareth Jones.
- ○ One video to watch: New Manager series on Lynda.com (LinkedIn Learning).
- ○ One account to follow: @harvard_business_review (Instagram).

Chapter 8
100 Pieces of Career Advice

The best pieces of career advice from the people who have inspired us

During our careers we have both been lucky enough to learn from, meet and work with some brilliant people. We have benefitted from these individuals sharing their stories, wisdom and advice with us at pivotal moments. They've been there when we needed a gentle push, when we felt more knotty than squiggly, and celebrated our successes along the way.

We have asked each person to share their best piece of career advice specifically for this book and in the context of squiggly careers. We've clustered the advice into key themes, and we hope you find their insights and pearls of wisdom as thought-provoking and inspiring as we have.

Stay true to yourself

1. Find a place to work where you can be yourself and look forward to going to work every day. This takes time and you will probably try a few things before discovering the right fit for you. And once you do find the right culture your attitude is so important. Be enthusiastic, positive and grab every opportunity you can to learn and grow.

   – Dame Carolyn McCall DBE, CEO, ITV

2. The best piece of advice that I got was from another poet, back when I was eighteen. It was twofold. He said that it takes many stars to decorate a sky, so focus on your own lights. That's become increasingly important to hold on to in this age of social media and mass data, where comparison has become that much easier to sink into. He then went on to say that every story is worth telling, every single one. The art is only in how well you tell it.

    – Sophia Thakur, Poet

3. Never stop dreaming.

    – Amelia Kallman, Futurist, Speaker and Author

4. Listen to all the advice you can, but your most powerful tool is your own filter for that advice. You know the situation better than anyone. Take counsel, take as much as you can – but then trust your own judgement.

    – Rosie Warin, CEO, Kin&Co

5. Find your superpowers and develop them.

    – Dan Gilbert, Founder, Brainlabs

6. Always allow your authentic self to shine in whatever career you decide, only then can your superpower emerge.

    – Adrian Walcott, Managing Director, Brands with Values

7. When deciding on a job move don't ever follow the money, or the interviewer, or the recruiter, or the advice of your friends. Only *you* really know the environment that will fill your soul with joy, the job that will have you bounding out of bed in the mornings, the challenge that will make your heart beat faster.

    – Sherilyn Shackell, Founder, The Marketing Academy

8. This piece of advice came from Nigella Lawson at a business event and has stayed with me ever since – she told us to 'be careful that you don't spend a lifetime climbing to the top of the ladder only to realize that it's against the wrong wall'. This reinforces the importance of getting really clear on choosing a career that matches your values and regularly

checking in on this so that you don't waste energy progressing in a field or job that doesn't truly fulfil you.

> – Alex McDonald, Founder, AM Wellness,
> Head of Content and Social, BUPA

9. Be really, really honest with yourself about what you do and don't value and what you want in your life. Your career choices should clearly help you achieve the things you want and avoid the things you don't. They need to allow you to celebrate your values not compromise them.

> – Tom Hampson, Marketing Director, Mamas & Papas

10. Life is lived forwards and understood backwards … My career looks well thought through but I have clear values and goals and this helps shape what I do and don't do.

> – Michele McGrath, Co-CEO, Brand Learning

11. You need to make conscious choices based on your priorities. As my career has progressed, company culture, my direct senior and my values have become more important. Never undervalue yourself. If you do, so will everyone else.

> – Carmen Rendell, Founder, Soulhub

Trust your gut

12. Trust your gut instinct. Your gut is your internal compass and you must learn to listen to it. You will have people all around you sharing their opinion on how you should be doing things, telling you which way to go. You must take on board their advice and guidance, but ultimately it is your own gut instinct that you should rely on to guide you through not only your career but your life.

> – Holly Tucker MBE, Founder, notonthehighstreet and Holly & Co

13. I think trusting your gut is often underestimated, particularly in technology, but we are actually the most sophisticated machines that exist. We take in billions of inputs a day and synthesize it into gut feelings – how incredible is that! I guess this is why Steve Jobs famously said 'intuition is more powerful than intellect'!

– Pip Jamieson, Founder, The Dots

14. Always trust your first instinct. Every time I have made a wrong call in business, it's because I chose to ignore my gut feeling.

– Robert Phillips, Founder, Jericho Chambers

15. Trust your instinct and act on it – have the courage to share the idea that sparks to life in a meeting or start the project that comes to you during the night. Trust that you've had that idea, thought or gut feeling for a reason and be bold enough to act on it. It's easy to go searching for the magic answers from someone or something else – the catalyst is remembering the magic answer is always within you.

– Jess Ratcliffe, Founder, Unleash Your Extraordinary

16. My biggest piece of advice is to listen to your intuition. Every single person that I loved and respected told me starting a business with a former Buddhist monk was insanity. They even staged an intervention. They gave me that advice because they loved me and wanted me to make the safe choice. The right choice never feels safe, it should feel scary, but mixed with the fear is a conviction that there is no other path. We all have that level of insight; it's whether we have the courage to listen to it. If not you, then who?

– Rich Pierson, Founder, Headspace

17. Never *ever* ignore your gut instinct. Don't compare yourself to anyone else. Invest in rest, self-awareness and a pastime or passion that has nothing to do with your career. Be kind to everyone regardless of their position. Own your mess-ups as much as your wins. And know that failure is where the magic happens if you are willing to see it. But above all else – be yourself.

– Caroline Casey, Founder, The Valuable 500

18. I believe that as a leader I am 'off course' 90 per cent of the time and that, much like driving a car, it is my continuous 2mm adjustments and interventions that keep me on the straight and narrow. The smallest of adjustments can alter your destiny.

– Jacqueline de Rojas CBE, President,
techUK, and Chair of the Board of Digital Leaders

Focus as much on 'how' you work as 'what' you do

19. The more skilled you become at something valuable, the more opportunities you'll begin to notice for high-impact work. If you're looking for your life's mission before you've taken the time to develop unambiguous abilities, you're unlikely to discover a truly remarkable path. Becoming so good you can't be ignored is often the first step towards a professional life rich with passion and meaning.

– Cal Newport, Author of *Digital Minimalism,*
Deep Work and *So Good They Can't Ignore You*

20. You build a reputation based on what you do, not what you say you're going to do. Delivery is everything. And don't forget no one has ever wished they spent more time in the office … Spend your time well.

– David Jones, Founder, You & Mr Jones

21. 'Live like nothing is above you or below you.' This has really shaped how I think about work. It makes me feel braver when I'm about to do something which feels like a leap, but it also reminds me that the way in which we do business and bring people with us on our work travels is just as important.

– Tash Walker, Founder, The Mix

22. Work hard, but don't be hard work.

– Rosie Brown, CEO, COOK

23. Having integrity in your work and in life will take you places. Be honest with your team, be honest with your clients, and be honest with yourself.

– Katee Hui, Founder, Hackney Laces

24. Go the extra click. We talk about going the extra mile, and that can seem daunting – especially to someone who has already given something their all. A click however? That's something small. Tiny. Achievable. Sending a CV? Go the extra click to find out one more thing about the person you're writing to. Reading some research in the trades? Click through to the source. It's tiny but I swear it makes such a difference – and you will stand out because of it.

– James Whatley, Strategy Partner, Digitas

25. When the shit hits the fan, some people step away and some people 'step up'. If you step up you will enjoy the chance to work outside of silos, find that normal rules about hierarchy and budget no longer apply, and see that it's the perfect time to make a difference: innovation, curiosity and creativity are rewarded. You can really stand out and change things in a shitstorm. So look for problems and be part of their solutions.

– Alex Cole, CMO, BUPA

26. Something that stuck with me after being mentored many years ago was the phrase 'Be cool on the net'. Often, we find ourselves in pretty heated situations (the Borough Market terror attack, or the Westminster attack for example). There are dozens of things going on at once. Raised voices, screaming and confusion are all around you. It's easy to get caught up. Emotion can creep in and before you know it, you're sounding panicked on the radio network. This in turn panics colleagues. Poor decisions are made. Fine motor skills perish. This can be disastrous for us. Even fatal. It's crucial to stay cool and calm when updating other team members and senior officers over the radio network, or when face to face. This helps keep colleagues calm and inspires confidence from your peers.

– Paul Robilliard, SCO19 Team, Metropolitan Police

27. You're always remembered by how you finish a role, not start one. No one adds value in their first month in a new job, it's about learning and finding your feet. However, the way you leave a job is the real test of character, you can add so much value in how you hand your old job over. It's your legacy to leave, so make sure you cross the I's, dot the T's and leave with integrity and your head held high.

– Kate Wall, Head of Advertising, KFC

28. You might not be the smartest person in the room. You might not be the most experienced and you may not be the most talented. But you can always be the most enthusiastic.

– Matt Cook, People and Brand Manager,
Gravity Road, and Founder, You Are Beautiful

Invest in your relationships

29. The inspiration for The AllBright was Madeleine Albright's famous quote, 'there's a special place in hell for women who don't help other women'. At AllBright we live by this mantra and everything we do is about celebrating women's successes. Our guiding principle is 'sisterhood works' and I would encourage women to start building their own work sisterhoods as early as possible in their career. The impact of a supportive peer network cannot be underestimated.

– Anna Jones, Co-founder, The AllBright

30. People are unlikely to care about your priorities unless you care about theirs. If you make sure someone can get away to pick their kids up from school, they will pay you back with interest.

– Jeff Phipps, Managing Director, ADP

31. Whatever career you end up in, make sure you obsess about
    your customers and your colleagues. Your understanding of and
    relationships with both will ultimately define your success
    because business is about relationships.

    – Dame Cilla Snowball CBE, Chair, Women's Business Council,
    Non-Executive Derwent London plc, previous Chairman
    and CEO of Abbott Mead Vickers

32. A dear friend and leadership coach once said to me, 'Be ruthless in your
    decision and humane in the execution.' I took this to mean … care
    about people. No matter what role you end up in … or difficult
    decisions you have to make, you can treat people with respect.

    – Anne-Marie McConnon, Chief Marketing Officer, BNY Mellon

33. Always look to be the right person for the team rather than the right
    person for the job.

    – René Carayol MBE, Leadership Speaker and Specialist

34. People divide into drains and radiators. Those who take your energy
    and those who give you energy. Surround yourself as much as you can
    with the radiators and the journey will be much more fun and much
    more productive.

    – Karen Mattison MBE, Co-founder, Timewise

35. Only employ people who are better than you and I challenge myself to
    do this every day.

    – Mark Boyd, Co-founder, Gravity Road

36. However possible, never fall out with any business colleagues, as you
    never know when your paths may cross in the future.

    – Judith Salinson, Trustee of NABS

37. The best thing you can say to your boss is, 'I'll take care of that for
    you'. If you make their life easier, you'll be the first person they think
    of for that next promotion.

    – Kate Bassett, Head of Content, *Management Today*

Have courage in your actions and decisions

38. I live by the words of Oscar Wilde: 'Shoot for the moon. Even if you miss, you'll land among the stars.' When it comes to work, 'good' is not good enough for me. I surround myself with passionate, enthusiastic, ambitious people who strive to be the best at what they do. Skills can be learnt, but energy, ambition and enthusiasm come entirely from you. I don't mind if we don't always hit the mark because when we aim for 'brilliant', our 'good' is pretty damn amazing too.

— Lisa Smosarski, Editor-in-Chief, *Stylist* Magazine

39. Stop asking for permission and prepare to ask for forgiveness instead. Chart your own course and remember that the biggest mistake you can make at work is to believe that the way things are is the way they have to be. Because all it takes to change the rules is for you to prove your new rules.

— Sam Conniff Allende, Author, *Be More Pirate*

40. It's better to look back on life and say, 'I can't believe I did that', than to look back and say, 'I wish I had done that'. Don't let time pass you by. Don't spend the rest of your life thinking about why you didn't do what you can do right now. Live your life. Take risks.

— Kanya King CBE, Founder, MOBO

41. As an entrepreneur the number one trait is being comfortable with uncertainty. Every day is likely to feel like a bit of a roller coaster full of ups and downs; take each experience as an opportunity to learn.

— Rajeeb Dey MBE, Learnerbly

42. Don't ever give up. As I have tried to persuade powerful institutions around the world that sustainability is the only game in town, I've been shouted at, ignored, insulted and on one occasion threatened with the law. But my unwavering conviction that a sustainable future is possible keeps me going. We all need to follow a passion. This planet of ours is mine.

– Sally Uren OBE, CEO, Forum for the Future

43. Everything is always OK in the end, so if it's not OK, it's not the end.

– Harriot Pleydell-Bouverie, Founder, Mallow & Marsh

44. Always say YES to opportunity and always remain true to yourself.

– Katie Kelleher, Crane Driver

45. I've discovered that you don't really grow unless you are really scaring yourself. Speaking for the first time in front of a big audience, working on a big project with ambitious goals or holding your own in front of a male-dominated Board, these take a willingness to step outside your comfort zone, test your mettle and discover just how well you can make an impact. So, fear fuels growth, makes you stronger and helps you to realize each step is big but not impossible. And sometimes, when you attempt such a step, you might fail, but you get up and try it again. That's resilience and determination.

– Edwina Dunn, CEO, Starcount

46. It is better to be wrong and interesting than right and boring.

– Daniele Fiandaca, Co-founder, Utopia and Token Man

47. It is better to regret something you have done than something you haven't done.

– Kate Straker, COO, Man AHL

48. Be brave. Ask the questions on your mind, put yourself in front of new opportunities, speak up when you think something needs to change. Nothing signals a leader like courage and integrity.

– Rachel Eyre, Head of Future Brands, Sainsbury's

49. Find a productive way to challenge the assumptions around you. They're everywhere, easily mistaken for truths, and suck you into the wrong choices very, very quickly.

– Adam Morgan, Founder, eatbigfish

50. Have the courage to leverage collective intelligence for success, and be open about that. It creates a more involved – therefore motivating – environment for your team, while giving you greater confidence in your course.

– Marina Haydn, Managing Director, *The Economist*

51. Be fearless and take risks. Be open to all the possibilities; don't rule things out because you think you're not good enough. Push yourself out of your comfort zone. Sometimes, that bit of fear can push you to rise to the challenge. You might just surprise yourself.

– Cindy Rose, CEO, Microsoft UK

52. Sheryl Sandberg says 'if you're offered a seat on a rocket ship … just get on'. This was the message that inspired me to make the best career decision I've ever made.

– Emma Roberts, Global Lead, Lean In Global Programmes

53. Making a significant career change requires courage. You need to be OK with failure if it doesn't work out and then almost not see it as a failure, because in reality you have still moved forward as you will have learnt a lot.

– Jonny MP, Photographer

54. Passion and nerve. In order to follow your ambition you need bucketloads of passion and nerve. Passion because you will have to exhibit your inner drive to overcome obstacles and nerve because you will be taking yourself out of your comfort zone.

– Lyndy Payne CBE, Honorary WACL Member

55. Feel the fear and do it anyway.

– Claire Hilton, Managing Director Brand and Insight, Barclays

Prioritize your learning

56. Early in your career, don't choose the job where you'll be happiest. Choose the job where you'll grow the most. Investing in learning is the most important career choice you can make. As your career develops, don't choose the job where you'll be happiest. Choose the job where you'll have the most impact. Knowing your job makes a difference is the strongest source of meaning at work.

– Professor Adam Grant, Wharton University,
Author of *Originals*, *Give and Take* and *Option B*

57. If you're feeling too comfortable in your job (you'll know that's true if you've stopped learning), then it's probably time to find something new that makes you feel uncomfortably excited. So stop worrying and take the leap if the opportunity excites you.

– Tim Chatwin, VP Communications and
Public Affairs, EMEA, Google

58. Always be learning. The world is changing so quickly, the most important skills you can have are adaptability, a learning mindset and an understanding of the technologies driving that change. Who is to say that spending eight hours a week on applied learning isn't more of a productivity gain than being in meetings or sending emails? Not to mention being more fun. Learning is now the job.

– Kathryn Parsons MBE, Co-founder and Co-CEO, Decoded

59. Invest in your own professional development – don't wait for your employer to do this for you. Being a lifelong learner is now a key employability skill. Research shows that over a thirty-year career, you'd need to update, refresh or completely retrain six times to stay relevant. A scary and sobering thought! With the pace of advancing digital technology moving at the speed it does, retraining and futureproofing your career couldn't be more important.

– Nikki Cochrane, Co-founder, Digital Mums

60. Aim to grow bigger than your job role. I believe one of your main aims should be to learn more, add more value and gain as much company and contextual experience to grow bigger than your job role. This way, it's more likely that you'll deliver beyond expectations, you'll be developing yourself as well as your career and you'll become the obvious person to take on a promotion should it arise. Don't stay in your box and seize the opportunities at hand.

– Jack Lowman, Senior Marketer and Author of Hack Yourself

61. Ask yourself three things: are you learning, earning enough, having fun? If you have two out of three think about how you can get all three. If you're getting one or zero it's time to do something different.

– Rebecca Crallan MD, Head of Cancer Intelligence, Cancer Research UK

62. Look after Number One. This doesn't mean throttle back on how generous you are with your time, but it's important to manage your career very actively and not wait for someone else to do that for you. The best way to do this is make it easy for others to give you feedback on your performance. I'm always surprised by how many people haven't really thought about this point. How easy do others find me to give feedback to? Do they rate me 10/10 or just 6/10? If it's the latter how can I nudge it up? Only you can manage this kind of improvement.

– Matt Kingdon, Co-founder, ?What If!

63. You can have it all in your career, just probably not at the same time. At Facebook we talk about people's careers as being like a 'jungle gym'. You have to navigate your way through the gym in whichever way works the best for you. And aim for continual improvement rather than perfection, that way you never stop learning.

– Carolyn Everson, VP Global Marketing Solutions, Facebook

64. Your career is the sum total of all the people you work with and learn from.

– Jon Rudoe, Advisor, Evolve Beauty

65. Be interested first and interesting second.

– Phil Gilbert, Director of Energy Solutions, E.ON UK

66. You owe it to yourself and those you work with to keep learning. When the learning stops, it's time to move on.

– Sarah King, Co-founder, Work.by Design

67. The journey of any good psychologist, or person, is as much learning *not* to know, as it is showing that you know. Only then can you be truly curious, surprised and inspired by another human being.

– Ben Hague MD, Psychologist

68. The best decision I ever made was to optimize my career for learning. Not salary or status or promotion or profession or any other proxy for career progress. I have simply flown in the direction of the steepest, most vigorous learning curve I could find and attacked it with everything I had. When the curve started to flatten, I sought ways to steepen it again. That hasn't meant I've always been successful – in fact it's probably meant I've failed more – but it has exposed me to a broad array of different challenges and experiences that have shaped who I am both personally and professionally.

– Rob O'Donovan, Co-founder and CEO, CharlieHR

69. Ask yourself this: does your working life give you interesting stories to tell your friends and family? If the answer is no, then maybe it's time for a change. Find a new role that ignites a childhood curiosity within you again, as it's through an inquisitive mindset that we learn new things, which keeps us interested and interesting.

– Tom Tapper, Co-founder, Nice and Serious

Design a career that works for you

70. Carve out your own path and focus on staying in your own lane. That doesn't mean totally putting your blinkers on, but it does mean not getting too distracted by what others are doing. Comparing yourself is very normal human behaviour, extremely hard to navigate or avoid, but turning comparison into inspiration is my biggest tool. Instead of asking 'Why does that person have that thing I want?' I think 'How cool, that person has made it work! What steps shall I take to get there too?'

– Emma Gannon, Author of *The Multi-Hyphen Method*,
Host of *Ctrl Alt Delete*

71. The advice of 'do what you love', while seeming appealing, can also create a burden on our own expectations. Not all of us can do a job that feels like our calling in life. For me the best advice for people in jobs is to be always looking for a way to do something closer to what excites you but not to beat yourself up about where you end up. When I started working at Google all I wanted to do was work on YouTube. There was no YouTube team so I started helping out in my lunchtimes. Sharing facts, gathering information, sending round interesting research that I found. When a job came up the UK boss of Google said, 'It seems to make sense that Bruce does this'.

– Bruce Daisley, VP Twitter EMEA
and Author of *The Joy of Work*

72. If you're not happy in your career, change something and get on a ladder worth climbing. And don't wait for the perfect time, do it before you're ready – time is the one thing you can't get back. So, don't let money dictate your career decisions, it's just one of the factors you should consider.

– Laurence McCahill, Co-founder, The Happy Startup School

73. If you have a career which is not 9–5 in its expectations don't make the mistake of dropping to four days a week. You will be paid 20 per cent less for the same amount of work. Find other ways to create the mix between work and home.

– Sara Bennison, Marketing Director, Nationwide

74. Pick a company that will challenge you intellectually instead of one that will pay you well. I actively chose worse-paying companies for more interesting and challenging roles and that's exactly what led to a rocket ship of personal development.

– Dan Murray-Serter, Founder, Heights

75. Research who you want to work for and why you want to work for them and work out how you can become indispensable to them.

– Tamara Cincik, Founder and CEO, Fashion Roundtable

76. When I'm thinking about career choices, I always ask myself whether something opens more possibilities in my future life or closes more down. Narrowing down isn't necessarily bad, but it needs to be done thoughtfully.

– Sarah Warby, CEO, Lovehoney,
and NED, MoneySuperMarket

77. Just get started. It's harder than ever to map out the perfect career path, so make the best start you can and keep on tweaking your ideas and ambitions until you find your way to the thing that works for you.

– Steven Watson, Founder, Stack Magazines

78. I strongly believe that an individual *must* take complete ownership and control over their own career journey. That's a non-negotiable term in achieving career success, in my opinion. Your career is 'yours' … not your company's, not your line leader's, not your mentor's, not your coach's, and not even your family members', friends' nor your peers'!

– Mark Brayton, Advisory Board Member, Save the Children UK

79. An important mindset change when embarking on the hunt for a new role is that *you* are interviewing a business just as much as they are interviewing you. Prepare accordingly and go in with three non-negotiables in mind that you know you need to feel happy, fulfilled and able to use your value to the best effect. Then ask questions to delve into whether the business can meet them.

– Clare Beaumont-Adam, Founder, Panda Bear Baby Company

80. Don't let a grand plan or ambition get in the way of making the right decision now. Ask yourself 'will this (new) job add more to my knowledge, skills and experience in the next two years than the one I am doing now?' and 'will I be able to do it well?' If the answer to both is a resounding yes – go for it!

– Justin King CBE, Former Chief Executive, Sainsbury's, Chairman, Wyevale Garden Centres and NED, Marks & Spencer

81. No one cares as much about your career as you.

– Amelia Torode, Founder, The Fawnbrake Collective

82. You will never know what you want to do, but if you ever find yourself doing what you don't want to do … get the hell out!

– Will Butler-Adams, CEO, Brompton Bikes

83. Don't limit yourself. A number of jobs and career opportunities may come your way, and however they show up, be present to the possibility of doing something new.

– David McQueen, Coach and Speaker

84. Be brave. We have a long career journey ahead. Change it up and reinvent yourself when the joy drifts out of what you are currently doing. We have multiple careers in all of us.

– Victoria Fox, Chief Executive, AAR

85. 'Make a decision and then make it work' – particularly useful to me as I am hopelessly indecisive and would agonize for hours over everything.

– Carrie Longton, Co-founder, Mumsnet

Make sure your time is well spent

86. Do the smallest and simplest thing you can do to start today. If you can't, ask someone who can.

– Lauren Currie OBE, Managing Director, NOBL

87. Start with the end in mind. You are ninety on a park bench looking back. What matters?

– Amanda Mackenzie OBE, CEO, Business in the Community

88. Do what you love and get clear on what that looks like for you. We can all easily get distracted in our exciting world and confuse 'busy' with productive. When I am not clear or focused, everything takes longer.

– Nicky Raby, Actor

89. Think about your time like an investor would about money. You have such a finite amount of time in your work/career and you need to always be considering: how am I making good things happen with my time investment – what is my impact – and how can I maximize what I get back out of it?

– Ben Tyson, CEO, Born Social

90. Unless you're a watchmaker, time is a very poor measure of your work. Especially in any career where the output of a role is thinking based. If you do just one great thing a day, that's a good day of work. It may have taken just a few moments of brilliance to achieve. If so, good on you. Because a day can be lost to so little.

– Mark Eaves, Co-founder, Gravity Road

91. Done is better than perfect. It can always be improved but if you wait until it is perfect you might miss your shot.

– Laura Mimoun, Founder, KALEIDO

92. Always communicate your progress and avoid over-promising. If you say yes to everything and deliver nothing, you will be seen as less reliable than the person who says nothing and delivers the same.

– Kate Rand, Director of People and Operations, Beyond

Look after yourself

93. Do all you can to keep things in balance – spiritual fulfilment and material reward, looking after yourself and others, building big relationships with colleagues and family and friends, playing to your strengths and stretching yourself, ambition for the future and enjoyment of the present. The secret lies in the use of the word 'and' – never let it become an 'or'.

– Andy Bird, Author of *The Inspired Leader*

94. Make your mental and physical health your number one priorities and ask yourself these questions regularly: am I learning? Am I growing? Am I recovering? Am I feeling purposeful? Am I feeling proud? Am I being kind? Am I experiencing joy?

– Michelle Morgan, Co-founder, Livity, and Founder, Pjoys

95. We spend an incredibly large proportion of our lives at work. If you want to live a fulfilled life then your work should be personal – there's no shame in that. If your relationship with your career doesn't feel vital or emotional, it's time to make a switch.

– Jack Graham, Founder and CEO, Year Here

96. You don't need to always have an answer. It's OK to say 'I don't know, but I'd like some time to go away and find out, and come back to you'. It's OK to sit and listen, and don't feel like you have to add something. It's OK to go back later, and say 'I've been contemplating on the discussion, and here are some thoughts'. Despite the breakneck pace of work, you can be the person who takes a breath before they speak, or the person who gives others the space to reflect and consider.

– Matthew Knight, Founder, Leapers

97. A note to self: breathe, access where you are, analyse what you're doing and smile at how far you've come.

– Adi Alfa, Presenter, Actress, Writer, Director

98. Following the 2008 financial crisis I noticed something very clear in our clients: those who showed resilience, tenacity and an ability to bounce back quickly were also the ones who had a robust passion for something outside of work. It was very stark. Those dedicating every brutal hour to 'the salvage mission' often seemed to make things harder for themselves and their businesses. So paint, sing, dance, bake, knit, run, read, hike, bowl, fish – whatever works. Career-wise these things are not a luxury; they are a necessity.

– James Healy, Gravitas and Presence Coach

99. Know what fuel you'll need. How to get to your destination, how to reach your goals, how to ensure you continue to make progress on the path you're on. What ingredients do you need today? What tools do you need, what environment do you need to work in, what kind of breaks do you need to take?

– Ian Sanders, Storyteller

100. In a creative practice there are moments where ideas connect and you can achieve clarity and a sense of real insight, but this is short-lived exhilaration that usually follows long periods of research, experimentation and more mundane work. I try not to focus only on completing works because that satisfaction is very fleeting. Being present within the moment of each incremental action of the process can lead to greater fulfilment. The main bit is in doing it, so find joy in that. The work is never really finished anyway.

– Max Warren, Silversmith and Lecturer, Central Saint Martins

And to finish, here are two pieces of career advice from us . . .

'Never live the
same year twice.'
– Sarah

'Run your
own race.'
– Helen

Acknowledgements

Amazing If is so much more than the two of us, so we want to thank everyone who has been part of our journey so far. This book has only been possible because of all the people, teams and organizations who have helped by testing, adapting and using our tools with us, and then at work. From those who came along to our very first launch event, to our supportive online community and our global clients prepared to take a punt on doing development differently, we are incredibly grateful to each and every one of you.

Combining writing a book with working and being mums to toddlers has been a challenging task! Our ever supportive partners, friends and family all rallied around us to make this book happen. And we want to give an extra special mention to Helen's husband, Gareth, and Sarah's partner, Tom. They gave us the space and time to write and put up with everything – from being weeks behind on the latest *Game of Thrones* episodes to holidays punctuated with writing days. You are both brilliant – thank you.

The squigglier our respective careers have become, the more we've enjoyed them. Practising what we preach has been a big part of this but so have the organizations we've worked in and the people we've worked with and for. We'd like to say a huge thank you to everyone who has been part of our careers so far and has inspired, challenged and motivated us to keep learning and growing. Our work is better because of you.

Our editor, Lydia, championed us and our book from the beginning. Her dedication extended to repeating every exercise in this book multiple times and the high standards she set for herself and us has, we think, made the promise of a great book into a reality. Lydia – we really couldn't have done this without you.

Finally, we'd like to thank each other. Writing a book with a best friend and business partner is potentially treacherous in all sorts of ways, but through the process we've seen each other's strengths in a new light. Helen's energy, perspective and positivity gave us the momentum to start and Sarah's creativity, consideration and commitment gave us the grit to get the book finished. We feel lucky we met all those years ago and we are excited to find out what the future holds as we continue on our mission to make work better for everyone.

Design Your Squiggly Career

Endnotes

1. https://www.thebalancecareers.com/common-characteristics-of-generation-x-professionals-2164682
2. https://www2.deloitte.com/content/dam/Deloitte/global/Documents/About-Deloitte/gx-dttl-2014-millennial-survey-report.pdf
3. https://www.forbes.com/2010/03/04/happiness-work-resilience-forbes-woman-well-being-satisfaction.html#2751be36126a
4. https://www.mckinsey.com/~/media/mckinsey/featured%20insights/future%20of%20organizations/what%20the%20future%20of%20work%20will%20mean%20for%20jobs%20skills%20and%20wages/mgi-jobs-lost-jobs-gained-report-december-6-2017.ashx
5. https://www2.deloitte.com/uk/en/pages/human-capital/articles/introduction-human-capital-trends.html
6. https://yougov.co.uk/topics/economy/articles-reports/2018/08/24/over-nine-ten-not-working-usual-9-5-week
7. Ibid.
8. https://www.wired.co.uk/article/we-work-startup-valuation-adam-neumann-interview
9. https://www.hrreview.co.uk/hr-news/strategy-news/5-signs-you-could-be-a-victim-of-leavism/111334
10. https://www.tuc.org.uk/news/15-cent-increase-people-working-more-48-hours-week-risks-return-%E2%80%98burnout-britain%E2%80%99-warns-tuc
11. https://news.harvard.edu/gazette/story/2017/04/over-nearly-80-years-harvard-study-has-been-showing-how-to-live-a-healthy-and-happy-life/
12. https://business.linkedin.com/talent-solutions/job-trends/purpose-at-work?src=gua
13. https://www.gallup.com/workplace/231605/employees-strengths-company-stronger.aspx

14. https://psycnet.apa.org/record/2005-08033-003
15. https://business.linkedin.com/content/dam/me/business/en-us/talent-solutions/resources/pdfs/global-talent-trends-2019-EMEA.pdf
16. https://www.gallup.com/workplace/231605/employees-strengths-company-stronger.aspx
17. https://www.lsbf.org.uk/media/2760986/final-lsbf-career-change-report.pdf
18. http://changingminds.org/explanations/values/values_development.htm
19. https://hbr.org/2019/03/to-seem-more-competent-be-more-confident
20. https://www.newyorker.com/science/maria-konnikova/social-media-affect-math-dunbar-number-friendships
21. https://www.independent.co.uk/news/business/news/business-ethnic-gender-diversity-performance-levels-better-study-workplace-office-mckinsey-a8166601.html
22. https://hbr.org/2011/01/the-real-benefit-of-finding-a
23. https://fs.blog/2014/10/adam-grant-give-and-take/
24. https://www.ft.com/content/0151d2fe-868a-11e7-8bb1-5ba57d47eff7
25. https://hbr.org/2014/08/curiosity-is-as-important-as-intelligence
26. https://hbr.org/ideacast/2018/10/the-power-of-curiosity
27. https://hbr.org/2012/01/creating-sustainable-performance
28. https://journals.sagepub.com/doi/pdf/10.1177/0002764203260208
29. https://www.businessinsider.com/microsoft-ceo-satya-nadella-on-growth-mindset-2016-8?r=US&IR=T
30. https://www.inc.com/jeff-haden/21-side-projects-that-became-million-dollar-startups-and-how-yours-can-too.html
31. https://www.ibm.com/services/learning/pdfs/IBMTraining-TheValueofTraining.pdf
32. https://hbr.org/2009/01/why-sleep-is-so-important.html
33. https://www.forbes.com/sites/daviddisalvo/2016/10/30/six-reasons-why-walking-is-the-daily-brain-medicine-we-really-need/#1ab5fa8352b8
34. https://www.telegraph.co.uk/education-and-careers/0/rising-epidemic-workplace-loneliness-have-no-office-friends/
35. https://www.theguardian.com/money/2016/jan/07/can-money-buy-happiness
36. https://news.gallup.com/businessjournal/182792/managers-account-variance-employee-engagement.aspx

Index